Beyond
the Birds
and the
Bees

Beyond the Birds and the Bees

Gregory K. Popcak, MSW, LCSW

Our Sunday Visitor Publishing Division
Our Sunday Visitor, Inc.
Huntington, Indiana 46750

To My Children.
May God grant them lives filled with His love.

Table of Contents

Introduction

Among the many difficulties parents encounter
today, . . . one certainly stands out: giving children
an adequate preparation for adult life, particularly
with regard to education in the true meaning of
sexuality.

— The Pontifical Council for the Family,
The Truth and Meaning of Human Sexuality

Last month, your three-year-old asked you, "But *how* do
babies get in their mommy's tummy?" Two weeks ago, your
five-year-old son wanted to know why daddy has hair "down
there" and he doesn't. Then there was last week, when your
eleven-year-old daughter went to the bathroom thinking she
had a stomachache, and suddenly began screaming in terror,
"Mom! Help! I'm bleeding!" Just yesterday, you found a copy
of *Playboy* under your thirteen-year-old son's mattress, and this
afternoon — though you don't know it yet — your fifteen-
year-old daughter is going to come home from school to tell
you that she has been asked out on her first date. *(Gasp! Clutch
heart. Thud.)*

While I sincerely hope that you will never have to deal with all of these issues at the same time, they raise an interesting question. In each of these cases, would you know how to respond in a loving, gentle, faithful way so that your children could learn — at your feet —how to become both sexually holy and sexually whole? Or would you start stammering and shifting in your place; your mouth dry, your palms sweaty, feeling slightly faint and desperately looking for either a stiff drink or a place to lie down — or perhaps both?

Either way, there is no aspect of parenting that is more emotionally charged and emotionally challenging than dealing with and respectfully nurturing your child's developing sexuality. I believe it is doubly difficult for Christian parents who — while wanting their child to develop his or her sexuality as fully as God intends — also want their child to appreciate the responsibility and spiritual significance that attends that sexuality.

Pardon Me, Is There a Superhero in the House?

I have always thought how wonderful it would be if there was a superhero that could guide us through such treacherous waters of parenting. Whenever a difficult parenting situation arose, like any of the ones that began this introduction, we could tune into the latest episode of *The Adventures of . . . FAMILY MAN!* (*"Faster than a runny nose! More powerful than two-ply toilet paper! Able to leap tall Lego towers in a single bound!"*) to marvel at how the caped wonder of family life would deftly resolve family problems with a flourish.

Alas, this is not to be. But I believe that with the proper tools, each parent can be FAMILY MAN! or SUPERMOM! to one's own children (the Boy and Girl Wonder). It is my hope that this book will be one of the tools that not only helps you sail over the crises that accompany your child's sexual development, but more importantly — to the degree that it is possible — prevent those crises from occurring in the first place.

But Do I Have to?

Of course, we all know that we are supposed to prepare our children for adulthood. In fact, the entire point of parenting is to prepare our children to have healthy, adult relationships (both with others and with the God who made them). When it comes to teaching our kids about sex, though, there is a part of each of us that wishes we could weasel out of the job.

The other day, I told a friend of mine that I was working on a book about talking to kids about sex. Now, my friend is a very solid Catholic who takes his faith seriously and works hard to live it out in his family life, but at this topic he started to smile ruefully and shake his head. "I'd like to see what you have to say about that." he said. " I was just talking about this with some of the people I work with." He added, only half-jokingly, " I know I can't do this, but there's a big part of me that wants to tell my kids to 'just go and learn it on the street like I had to.' My parents *never* talked about sex. Are you kidding me? I don't even know where to start."

Of course, my friend wasn't entirely serious, but his comments raise some excellent questions. Do we really have to teach our children about sex? Can't the schools do it? Can't they just learn it on their own? Or better still, won't their healthy, Christian sexuality just blossom on its own if I keep them in a bubble and never tell them anything?

I hope the answers to these questions are obvious (just in case, they are "yes," "no," "no," and "no."), but to be sure, let's see what the Church has to say on the subject.

Sex education, *which is a basic right and duty of parents*, must always be carried out under their attentive guidance, whether at home or in educational centers chosen by them. In this regard, the Church reaffirms the law of subsidiarity, which the school is bound to observe when it cooperates in sex education, by entering into the same spirit that animates the parents. [emphasis mine]

— *Familiaris Consortio*

So the jury is in. The Church says that as far as the sexual education of your children is concerned, "You have the right to do it!" Of course, with this right comes certain responsibilities. As parents, we need to form our consciences properly regarding sexual ethics, and also to educate ourselves as to the best methods of nurturing our children's sexuality. To help you in this process, I offer the following ten points you'll need to keep in mind as you read through *Beyond the Birds and the Bees*. We will develop these points much more fully throughout the book, but I want you to know from the outset what to look for and keep in mind as you read through the chapters that follow. Likewise, each of the following points are either suggested by or taken directly from *The Truth and Meaning of Human Sexuality* (cf. section 6.1).

Ten Tips for the Teacher (That Means You)

1. All children are different with regard to their level of maturity and intellectual capacity. It is up to you, as parents, to be sensitive to the level of *each* of your children (i.e., avoid "cookie-cutter" methods, please) when sharing information about sexuality.

2. Generally speaking, it is the father's primary responsibility to teach/model healthy sexuality to his sons and it

is the mother's primary job to teach/model healthy sexuality to her daughters. This is not an exclusive responsibility, however, as each parent has something important to teach each child regardless of gender. Even so, each parent must never forget his or her duty to be a good example and teacher of what it means to be a Christian man or woman.

3. When talking about sex, we should always take care to connect it to its spiritual and moral dimensions. Sex is something that involves the whole spiritual, emotional, and physical person. It is not enough to give mechanical information. We must teach our children how to have an integrated sexuality.

4. When correcting our children for inappropriate sexual comments, self-touching, or other behaviors, it is not enough to say "Don't do that!" We must avoid using corrective measures that give the impression that sex is something that is bad or to be feared. We must always give sensitive, moral explanations for why the behavior is wrong *and be able to explain why the moral alternatives we are offering are better for the child's body, mind, soul, and relationships.* This last point is of absolute importance.

5. It is not enough to simply give information about sex and morals. We must be willing to serve as patient examples, teachers, and confidantes to our children on an ongoing basis. As our children's sexuality unfolds, we must play an active role at each stage, providing guidance and assistance. We must work to be sensitive and credible authorities on sexual matters in our children's eyes.

6. We must teach our children to have a healthy respect for their own bodies, minds, and souls, and to have

genuine respect for the bodies, minds, and souls of the people God puts in their path.

7. The goal of all discipline should be teaching the child self-discipline. We must give children the tools they need to evaluate their surroundings from a loving and faith-filled perspective.

8. Chastity is not the same thing as repression. We must teach our children about the power, strength, and joy that come from self-mastery, and how the choice to be chaste increases their chances of having a happier marriage, a healthier life, and a more beautiful soul.

9. Parents cannot do it all on their own. We must be willing to accept competent help from qualified sources. This includes reading good books on the subject of sexuality, and being willing to consult with experts in education, psychology, theology, and child development when the need arises.

10. In everything we do and teach, we must always keep in mind that God is working alongside us. His grace empowers us and our children to grow in virtue every day, and His mercy is there for us when we fail. Through prayer, and participation in the sacraments, we must constantly seek the Lord's guidance, and teach our children to do the same.

The above ten points represent a pretty tall order, but I promise that we will explore these themes throughout the book and give you many tools to help you make these ideals a reality.

How to Use This Book

To help you raise your children to be both sexually whole and sexually holy, *Beyond the Birds and the Bees* will combine a faithfully Catholic perspective with current research on psychology and child development to help you find answers to questions like the following:

- What does a healthy Catholic sexuality look like?
- How can you have age-appropriate conversations about sex with your child?
- What lessons must children learn at each stage to develop a healthy Christian sexuality?
- How can you teach your child what it takes to be a true Catholic man or woman?
- How can you help your children have healthy, Christian dating relationships?
- What steps can you take to help your child exhibit moral courage and sexual chastity?
- What do you need to do to prepare your young adult for marriage? — and much more.

This book is divided into two sections. Part One will help to develop your own understanding of the Catholic vision of love and prepare you to pass that vision on to your children through your daily interactions and conversations with them. Likewise, the last chapter in it (chapter three) will use the acronym RESPECT to illustrate the seven principles of having age-appropriate discussions about sex with your children.

Part Two will take you step-by-step through the ages and stages of childhood, beginning with infancy and continuing all the way through adolescence. In each of these chapters, you will discover what the major goals and concerns of each stage are, and learn how to face those goals and concerns with faith, love, and grace. Once we have made it through the various stages of childhood, we'll have a chapter specially reserved for addressing sensitive sexual questions that did not figure prominently in the rest of the book. Here, we'll explore such issues as when and how to talk about abortion, what — if anything — you should teach your child about artificial birth control, how to sensitively and faithfully handle questions surrounding the issue of homosexuality, and what you need to know about sexual abuse and other issues. Each of these topics will be handled in a practical, sensitive, orthodox manner that will help you respond to your child's questions with loving confidence.

Having addressed the basic outline of the book, I think it is likewise important to explain the one thought that underlies everything else you will read in these pages. Specifically, that every parent and child needs to realize that sexuality is bigger than "the birds and the bees." We cannot reduce sexuality to "the marital act." We must not think of sexuality as a merely physical thing; neither may we confine our understanding of Christian sexuality to the bedroom. As the Vatican points out in *The Truth and Meaning of Human Sexuality*, "sexuality is not something purely biological; rather it concerns the intimate nucleus of the person." According to the Church, sexuality is not just something that you express through lovemaking (although it is that too). More importantly, your sexuality is a representation of *who you are* and how well your whole personhood (that is, your emotional, mental, spiritual, and relational well-being) is formed. Sexuality, like intelligence or creativity or spirituality, is what psychologists call a "construct." That is, it is a label that represents several other qualities all rolled into one. Let me give you an example.

Think about your favorite cake. That cake is a "construct." In other words, it is a thing that is "constructed" of flour, sugar, milk, eggs, oil, flavoring, energy (heat), and all the other individual ingredients that make it up. When you talk about your cake you also refer, indirectly, to the unique combination of ingredients that go together to make that cake so good. In the same way, sexuality is a "construct" — a recipe — made up of several different ingredients, namely: Love, Responsibility, Joy, Respect, Cooperation, Spirituality, Intimacy (verbal and emotional communication), and Personhood. Of course, fostering your child's sexuality includes teaching your child the biological facts of reproduction and the skills of self-discipline, but it is so much more. Fostering your children's sexuality really means teaching your children — through word and example — how to be loving, responsible, joyful, respectful, cooperative, spiritual, communicative, fully functioning human *persons* from the day they emerge from the womb, so that when you finally do have "the talk," everything will fall into place. The fact is, if you try to teach your child about sex itself without having at least made significant headway into establishing these virtues in your children's life, your children's sexuality will be disordered no matter what you tell them. In the next chapter, we'll take a closer look at each of those virtues, but for now it is enough to know that when I talk about nurturing your child's sexuality, I am really talking about what it takes to raise up children who can become godly men and women.

Having said that, I would encourage you to think of this book as a companion volume to *Parenting with Grace: The Catholic Parent's Guide to Raising (almost) Perfect Kids* (Our Sunday Visitor), which I co-authored with my wife and partner, Lisa Popcak. Though I will be looking at sexuality exclusively in this book, I hope you can understand why I would think of this as an artificial separation. Since nurturing your child's sexuality is really about building your child's character (albeit in a sexual sphere), all of the methods and parenting goals my partner and I outline in *Parenting with Grace* can and should be applied to the topic at hand. Likewise, if you would like to understand a little bit more about what it means to celebrate a deeply satisfying, remarkably joyful and profoundly Catholic sexuality in your own marriage, you may wish to take a look at *For Better...FOREVER! A Catholic Guide to Lifelong Marriage.* Because I firmly believe that we cannot give what we do not have, this latter book can help make sure the sexuality you celebrate in your marriage is both whole and holy, empowering you to pass a healthy sexuality on to your children. But whether or not you have any interest in these other titles, I believe that you will find many helpful, practical ideas for raising children in the chapters that follow.

Is It Too Late to Start?

One final concern. Considering the developmental approach we take in *Beyond the Birds and the Bees,* some readers might be wondering if they are too late if they didn't start on the day their children sprang forth from the womb. Rest assured, at whatever stage you've come to this book, you're just in time. Regardless of when you actually discovered the methods and ideas presented in the following chapters — methods and ideas which have their foundation in Church teaching and solid psychology — it is never too late to begin teaching your children how to have a healthy, godly sexuality. Whether your children are still in diapers or they are getting ready to say "I do," it is my hope that you will find validation for the terrific work you are already doing as a Christian parent, as well as more tips, techniques, and skills to help you raise great kids who know what it takes to be both sexually whole and sexually holy.

Part One:

A Recipe for Success

Are your own sexual attitudes both as healthy and holy as they could be? What does teaching your kids about sex really entail? Is it enough to give them "the talk"? What are the key personality ingredients needed to live out the Catholic ideal of love? The first part of *Beyond the Birds and the Bees* — comprising Chapters One through Three — answers these questions and more.

CHAPTER ONE

Pat-a-Cake, Pat-a-Cake, Baker's Man . . .

The Ingredients of a Healthy, Holy Catholic Sexuality

Married for twelve years, Dean and Sharyn have four children. Neither Dean nor Sharyn felt that their own sexual education had been healthy. Sharyn, a cradle Catholic, told me that her parents were very religious, but were uncomfortable talking about sex except to say, "Don't do it." Sharyn had a very sheltered childhood that was more or less shattered when she went to college, where she found she was ill-equipped to resist the culture of sex that saturated campus life. She became moderately sexually active and, in many ways, felt freer than she had before, having grown up in what she considered to be a "fairly oppressive atmosphere." She drifted away from the Church.

After college, her sex life cooled off as she focused on finding work and settling into adulthood. Almost on a lark she returned to Mass one Sunday after several years away. Liking what she found in her local parish, she became active in the music ministry, becoming a regular at Sunday Mass and even the odd weekday. When she met Dean, she wanted to have a different kind of relationship with him than she had had with other men in the past. She explained that she wanted to wait until marriage to have sex, and Dean seemed to re-

spect her for this. They were not able to stick to this plan completely, though, and were sexually active during their engagement. Even so, she continued to be more serious about her faith and learn more about what and why the Church teaches what it does about sexual ethics. In hindsight, Sharyn sees the wisdom of the Church's teaching and would like to pass on a more mature, faith-based understanding of sexuality to her children than she received from her own parents.

Dean's parents were more liberal, but no more helpful when it came to helping him understand how to properly form his own sexuality. As Dean explained, "My parents tended to have a 'boys-will-be-boys but just make sure to be careful' attitude — if you know what I mean."

Dean dropped out of the Church in young adulthood, but experienced a "reversion" (a reawakening of his spiritual life in the Church) a few years after he and Sharyn were married. Even though they were both Catholic, they still struggled to understand and apply the Church's teaching on sexual morals. As Dean put it, "I mean, I want our kids to be good kids, and I want them to see their Faith as an important part of their lives, but I don't want them to feel ashamed of their sexuality. Is there really a way to raise them to be faithful and healthy?"

Before beginning any journey, it's important to know where we're going. In the same way, if we Catholic parents are going to set out to raise sexually whole and holy kids, then we'd better be prepared to explain what it means to exhibit a healthy, *Catholic* sexuality.

Of course, there are those cynics who would suggest that there is no such thing as a healthy, Catholic sexuality. Those cynics are wrong, but in all fairness, their confusion can be easily understood.

As I was growing up, it seemed to me that Catholics fell into two "schools" when it came to sexual attitudes. The first was the "Keep-God-Out-Of-My-Bedroom School," which tends to maintain a more *laissez-faire* relationship between faith and fornication, essentially believing that as long as I occupy my mind with spiritual thoughts and attend Mass regularly, it doesn't matter if I meet my mistress for brunch afterward.

Then, there is the ever-popular "Aunt McGillicuddy's Antique Urn School" of human sexuality. This second group of individuals grudgingly admit that sex is beautiful — albeit in a somewhat grotesque, gothic sort of way — but more importantly, sex is seen as something that should be approached *cautiously*, *delicately*, and ideally, *infrequently* — like Aunt McGillicuddy's antique urn. (*"Don' you be fussin' with THAT now, missy! We only touch it if we have to dust it, and then, only once a month er sooo!"*)

Imagine my surprise, then, when I discovered that both of the above positions have actually been condemned as heresies by the Church (they represent forms of Gnosticism and Jansenism respectively) throughout the centuries. It was only after I began studying theology in college (and during a brief stint in the seminary) that I learned the truth about Catholic sexuality: specifically, that true Catholics do not ignore sex, or fear sex, but rather celebrate it as one of the most beautiful and profound "goods" God has given us. As the Vatican tells us in *The Truth and Meaning of Human Sexuality*, "Human sexuality is . . . part of the created gift which God saw as *very good*, when he created the human person in his image and likeness [emphasis in original]."

In my studies, I discovered — among other things — the sexual imagery that underlies the Eucharist, in which Christ enters us, body, soul, and divinity, and unites us to Him in the most intimate of embraces. I finally understood that when I went to Benediction and gazed upon the Blessed Sacrament exposed to me in all its radiance, I was actually staring into the eyes of my Divine Lover. I learned that the Song of Songs in Scripture was a not just a story of the passionate love between a man and a woman, but also a symbol of the passionate love God has for each of us. I was taught that every time a married couple made love, they were physically restating their wedding vows to each other — in fact, they were celebrating the sacrament of marriage. I was amazed to learn that the Church holds that sex, because of its power to unite, create, and perfect, actually serves a sacramental function in the context of marriage, and that by prayerfully contemplating the intimate union between a man and a wife, we can get a glimpse of what it will be like to be united with God when we go to heaven and celebrate our Eternal Wedding Feast with our Divine Lover.

Catholic sexuality, I have come to appreciate, is a profound and joyful thing. It is superior to what any other philosophy of sex has to offer because it insists that we respect the gift of our own humanity, as well as the humanity of our lover, and compels us to appreciate the power that we invoke when we share ourselves with that one person God has chosen for us. Furthermore, as I suggested earlier, Catholic sexuality is really about the communication of one whole person to another — with all that means! To exhibit a healthy Catholic sexuality, then, means to be a healthy, faithful person who knows how to communicate the fullness of his being to another healthy, faithful person. Who wouldn't want to celebrate a sexuality based on such a reality? Keeping this in mind, I would like to devote the remainder of this chapter to the eight virtues that stand at the heart of Catholic sexuality, and indeed, that stand at the heart of any human being who seeks both wholeness and holiness.

Flour Power!

The Eight Secrets of a Whole (and Holy) Catholic Sexuality

In the introduction, I compared human sexuality to a cake and asked you to think of the eight virtues that stand at the heart of Catholic sexuality as the "ingredients" that go into that cake. For the rest of this chapter, I'd like to outline the baking directions as well as offer some tips for how to prepare your ingredients. But first, the recipe.

In a loving home, mix . . .

1 cup Love (for best results, use self-donative variety)

1 cup Responsibility (mix 1/2 cup self-discipline with 1/2 cup stewardship)

1 cup Faith

1 cup Respect (combine 1/2 cup self-respect & 1/2 cup respect for others)

1 cup Intimacy (combine equal parts verbal and emotional communication)

1 cup Cooperation

1 cup Joy

1 cup Personhood (combine a sense of being made in the image of God with a heaping tablespoon of — choose one of the following — masculinity or femininity).

Bake until young adulthood.

Frost after wedding.

As you look at that recipe, some of you might be wondering why I have not included chastity in the mix. Well, the reason that chastity is not *in* the mix is that chastity *is* the mix. Many people are under the mistaken impression that chastity is the same thing as repression (all those jokes about "chastity belts" haven't helped matters in this regard). But chastity is really the ability to apply all of the virtues I mentioned above in the sexual sphere. I can say that I am chaste, not if I simply keep my genitals under lock and key, but rather if I know how to be loving, responsible, respectful, intimate, cooperative, joyful, faithful, and fully human in relationship to my sexuality. In other words, when I talk about being sexually whole and sexually holy, I am really referring to what the Church herself (as opposed to popular culture) calls chastity.

Having dealt with that issue, let's take a look at each of these virtues. First, because you can't give what you don't have, I would like to ask you to consider how good you are at expressing all of these virtues, both in your everyday life and your sexual relationship with your partner. The following quiz can help you identify those areas you are strong in, and those areas, which may require some shoring up.

Baker's Quiz

(Answer T or F to each of the following questions)

The following questions address each of the identified virtues in general, not simply in the sexual area of your life. Think about your relationship as a whole with your mate when you answer them, not just your genital/sexual relationship with your mate. Incidentally, the following quiz is not intended to be a comprehensive diagnostic measure of your true capacity for each of the eight virtues. Better to think of it as a kind of examination of conscience to see how well you manifest the qualities that define Catholic sexuality in your own life. Finally, if you aren't sure whether to answer true or false, ask your mate's opinion.

Directions: Give yourself one point for each statement you mark "True."

Love (Self-donative)

___ I am mindful of the goals and values that are important to my partner, and every day I work to help him/her meet his/her needs.

___ I willingly and cheerfully take on the challenges, responsibilities, and sacrifices of marriage and family life.

___ My mate would agree that I am an attentive, sensitive, generous, and thoughtful spouse.

___ My spouse and family get the best of me (as opposed to what's left of me after I am done with my work, friends, community involvements, and hobbies).

___ I willingly and generously respond to my mate's requests and needs, even the ones that make me uncomfortable (assuming they don't violate my moral standards).

___ I do not belittle or criticize the things or interests that my spouse enjoys but that I myself do not appreciate. Instead, I work to find the truth, goodness, and beauty in all the things my mate finds true, good, and beautiful.

Self-Donative Love score _____ *out of a possible six points.*

Responsibility (1/2 cup self-discipline; 1/2 cup stewardship)

___ I am good at delaying gratification in any area of my life (i.e., I don't whine and make everyone around me miserable) if circumstances require me to wait or "Do without" for a time.

___ I am attentive and responsive to the needs of my spouse and family, even if I don't always feel like it.

___ I clean, maintain, and care for the things God has given me, but not to the degree that people are afraid to use the things God has given me (e.g., "Welcome to my home — but don't touch anything!").

___ I am good at both expressing my emotions and controlling them, and I know the appropriate times to do either.

___ I am good at keeping my priorities in order (I do not feel pulled in a million different directions all of the time).

___ I am good at balancing meeting my own needs with meeting the needs of others.

Responsibility Score _____ *out of a possible six.*

Faith

___ I am attentive to the spiritual dimensions of everyday life.

___ I have an active prayer life that consists of formal and casual prayer, as well as regular participation in the sacraments.

___ I am able to discern God's speaking to me through the events of my everyday life.

___ I seek to live my life according to Scripture and the teachings of the Church, and I constantly strive to develop a deeper understanding/appreciation of both.

___ I have a faith that is both emotionally experienced and intellectually sound.

___ I am capable of explaining and defending the teachings of the Church in rational, meaningful ways.

Faith Score _____ *out of a possible six.*

Respect (1/2 cup self-respect ; 1/2 cup respect for others)

___ I am capable of making other people take me seriously.

___ I do not do things that will demean my God-given personal dignity or threaten my moral well-being, even if someone I care about gets irritated with me for taking that position.

___ I do not refuse the requests of others lightly. I do not refuse people simply because I do not feel like doing what they have asked. I respond to all requests that I believe are reasonable, and I give at least a fair hearing to those requests that are suspect to me before deciding how to respond.

___ I expect all members of my family to do as much as they are able to take care of our home and one another. I am good at making this happen.

___ I dress in a way that is attractive to others, but not provocative.

___ I make sure to tell the people I love how special and important they are to me every day, and to show that specialness in my behavior toward them.

Respect Score _____ *out of six points.*

Intimacy (combine equal parts verbal and emotional communication)

___ I am good at *respectfully* expressing my feelings.

___ My spouse would say that I am a good listener.

___ I am interested in learning about the things that are important to my mate, even if they don't interest me in the same way.

___ I regularly talk to my mate about my thoughts, opinions, and ideas.

___ My spouse would agree that I am an affectionate person.

___ I am sensitive to my mate's feelings, and I know how to respond in an appropriate, helpful way when (s)he is angry, sad, hurt, or even joyful.

Intimacy Score _____ *out of six points.*

Cooperation

___ My spouse would agree that I am an effective and respectful problem-solver.

___ I work well with my mate on many different projects.

___ My mate would agree that we work well together to keep our home and raise our children.

___ I am good at steering arguments and disagreements to a respectful and mutually satisfying resolution.

___ I regularly initiate discussions about future plans with my mate, and I am good at working with him/her to make sure those plans actually materialize.

___ My mate would agree that I consistently take him/her into consideration when making plans and decisions about allocating my time and energy.

Cooperation Score ___ *out of six points.*

Joy

___ I am able to marvel at God's hand in simple, everyday things.

___ I am comfortable being silly and playful.

___ I am in touch with my senses and am passionate about experiencing life through all of them.

___ My mate would agree that I have a healthy, respectful, and engaging sense of humor.

___ I enjoy surprises.

___ I love discovering new things and exploring new places and ideas.

Joyfulness Score _____ *out of six.*

Personhood

___ I know in my heart that I am made in the image and likeness of God, and I strive to exhibit *all* the virtues and qualities (like rationality, emotionality, nurturance, communicativeness, passion, creativity, wisdom, etc.) that make me *fully human.*

___ I know that God created my body, am pleased with the body God has given me, enjoy caring for my body and health, and feel competent with the use of my body.

___ I am not embarrassed or squeamish about my bodily functions.

___ I do not stop myself from developing certain skills, virtues, or strengths simply because I believe that "men/women aren't supposed to think/act/feel like that."

___ I do not believe that "Men are from Mars and Women are from Venus." Rather, I understand the Church's teaching that being "masculine" or "feminine" refer to living out all of the virtues which make me human *through the body God has given me.*

___ I know that I am a son or daughter of the Most High God. I understand the privileges to which that entitles me (in this life and the next), and I accept the responsibilities (living a moral, God-centered life) that accompany my God-given nobility.

Personhood Score ____ *out of six.*

Summary of Scores.

Write your totals for each section in the blanks below, then total the scores for a picture of your overall sexual health.

Self-Donative Love	_____	Responsibility	_____
Faith	_____	Respect	_____
Intimacy	_____	Cooperation	_____
Joy	_____	Personhood	_____

Total Score _____ *out of a possible 48 points.*

Well, How'd You Do?

Hopefully, having completed the preceeding quiz, you have a better sense of the strengths and weaknesses in your own sexuality. But chances are, as you read through the items, you had several questions. For example: you may have wondered what some of the items had to do with sexuality. Or, perhaps, if you scored lower in one section or another, you may be curious about how you could increase the presence of that trait in your life. Alternatively, you may be wondering what steps you can take to ensure that your children will be able to exhibit all of these qualities, both in their life, and in their sexuality.

Fear not, intrepid reader, for the best is yet to come.

In the next portion of the chapter, we are going to answer each of those questions. Plus, using the items on the quiz, I will offer you an outline for fostering a healthy, holy sexuality for yourself and your children.

Let's Start at the Very Beginning, a Very Good Place to Start . . .

Let's go back to the beginning of the quiz and work our way through this outline one exciting step at a time.

Self-Donative Love

The term "self-donation" figures prominently in the writings of Pope John Paul II when he talks about marriage and family life. Self-donation is love, but it is a special kind of love that empowers us to use our bodies, minds, and souls to work for the good of others, even while being mindful of our own God-given dignity.

The person who is accomplished at self-donation has the ability to make others feel loved and attended to. He knows how to be loving (defined as "working for the good of another") even when he does not feel like it, even if the person being loved does not always deserve such generosity. In short, self-donative persons are cheerful, thoughtful, loving, and generous. And yet, they are *able to do this without being a doormat*, without allowing themselves to be victimized or unreasonably taken advantage of by others. They are able to balance these two things (generosity and the need to set boundaries) because they are guided by a deep sense of their own God-given worth, and the God-given worth of those put in their path.

Obviously, the ability to practice self-donative love is extremely important in the sexual sphere. Self-donation prepares a person to do whatever is best for oneself and one's lover at any given moment, whether that means giving all of oneself, or holding something back because the time is not yet right to give it (just as God, who is completely self-donative, does not reveal all of himself and all of the blessings he wants to give us at once). Perhaps even more importantly, a truly healthy, Christian sexuality is founded on the belief that lovemaking is the fullest expression of how well, lovingly, and respectfully the lovers care for one another — not just in the bedroom, but all day long. Self-donation is the virtue that allows couples to say about their sex life, "See how well we care for each other all day long. And then at night, even our bodies work for each other's good!"

If you would care to increase the presence of self-donation in your marriage and family life, try the following.

(1) Develop a Family Mission Statement.

To help facilitate self-donation in yourself and your children, I recommend the use of a family mission statement. Essentially, this is a list of the virtues you wish to emphasize in the everyday life of your family, and a plan for practicing those virtues. For example, if you wanted to emphasize faith, joy, respect, and service in your family, you might make sure to: (a) "As a family, go to confession twice a month"; (b) "Have one evening a week for 'family time' where we play games or do projects together"; (c) "Speak respectfully when we make requests of one another (parents and children)"; (d) "Look for ways to help each other out without being asked," respectively.

A family mission statement is one way to pass on the idea to your children that it is their job to do all they can to work for the good of the other members of the family, regardless of their age and regardless of how they feel at any given moment. This is an important skill for marriage, as it directly affects people's ability to put the needs of another over their own feelings. In fact, it is exactly this ability to put the needs of another over our immediate wants or feelings that makes self-donation so important to sexuality. Find more specific assistance on how to develop your own family mission statement, in *Parenting with Grace: The Catholic Parent Guide to Raising (almost) Perfect Children.*

(2) Practice a Generous Spirit of Service.

One of the rules that I encourage families to practice is that those who trip over messes first should clean them up whether they made them or not. This encourages family members (both parents and children) to always look for opportunities to serve one another.

While this may only seem tangentially related to sexuality, one has to remember that sexuality is really an expression of one's whole character. Since this is the case, the ability to have a loving, attentive, respectful servant's heart is the hallmark of a truly godly lover, both in and out of the bedroom. In fact, one recent psychological study documented that the degree to which a married couple reported their sexual relationship to be satisfying (that is, both respectful and pleasurable) was directly related to how well the couple felt they worked together to complete housekeeping and child-rearing tasks.

Another way to encourage generosity in your marriage and your family life is to insist that each member of the family (parents and children) works hard to see the truth, goodness, and beauty in all the things each family member finds true, good, and beautiful. If you like art, Mexican food, monster truck rallies, football, ballet, or the color yellow and I don't, I could pick on you for liking those things, or at the very least, give you a wide berth when you attempt to pursue those interests. Alternatively, I could be generous to you and try to foster some appreciation for those things, mainly because I love you and I want you to feel that you can share the things that are important to you with me. I may never learn to have the same appreciation for the things you enjoy, but because I regularly and generously participate in the activities and interests you have, you will feel that I respect you, am interested in your life, and truly want to be your friend. Compare this to those marriages where husbands and wives have best friends who are not their mates (because "My wife can't stand when I talk about . . ." or "My husband would rather set himself on fire than join me in . . .") and you begin to understand the importance generosity plays in helping a couple celebrate a truly intimate marriage.

As far as fostering your children's sexuality goes, by modeling generosity in your marriage and encouraging your children to follow your good example, you teach your children that the most important thing persons can do is not to satisfy themselves, but to find satisfaction in working for the good of those around them.

(3) Make sure family is your priority.

We all struggle to balance the many responsibilities that tug at us every day. But true self-donation requires us to first attend to the people God has directly entrusted to our care. We cannot give the best of ourselves to friends, co-workers, and community, and give the leftovers to our families. This is the antithesis of the self-donation expected of a married person.

Likewise, the lessons for poor family priorities begin early. In an effort to see that our children are properly "socialized," we enroll them in thirty thousand activities, all on Wednesday. While socialization with friends and in the community is important, it cannot be so important that it turns family life into the place where we stop off on the way to something more interesting. This attitude violates self-donation because it teaches children to give only what's left over to the family.

To maintain your priority for your family and balance all of the other responsibilities in your life, use the following formula as a guide.

    a. Think of a week in the recent past when you could say that your family was functioning at its best. (Marriage solid. Kids basically compliant. Good rapport all around.) Now ask yourself, "How much time did we spend playing, talking, and working together that week?" The answer to this question is the amount of time your marriage and family require to run well.

b. There is a line that exists between fulfilling our obligation to give our employers a full day's work, and our need to stroke ourselves by making the most money or being the best-loved employee. How much time and energy does it take to give your employee a full day's work (and meet my financial needs) without stepping over that line where I am working for wealth and my own glorification? That is the amount of time to give to your work.

c. Now add the two amounts from "a" and "b" together. This represents the amount of time in your week that should be devoted to your work and family. Feel free to divide whatever is left over among friends, hobbies, and community-service projects.

The same applies to your children. Once you have established how much time it takes for your family to run well, and how much time and energy it takes for them to do well at school, whatever is left over can be given to hobbies, sports, friends, and other activities.

By using this formula, you model and teach how to guard the priority of your family, affording opportunities to practice self-donation to build a "community of love." Next, let's examine the next ingredient of a healthy, Christian sexuality — responsibility.

Responsibility (1/2 cup self-discipline; 1/2 cup stewardship)

Responsibility is the virtue that helps us decide how best to respond to our circumstances; to conduct ourselves with dignity, to nurture the people, and to maintain the things God has blessed us with. Responsibility has everything to do with sexuality because it encourages us to practice self-mastery, it tells us to treat other people with the dignity that they deserve, and it causes us to become trustworthy so that others can feel safe being vulnerable around us.

To increase the amount of responsibility you display in your family, practice self-discipline. Discourage whining in yourself and your children when you can't have what you want. Set goals and work toward them. Practice discipline that encourages self-monitoring in your children as opposed to discipline that requires you to be your children's conscience, policeman, and warden. Look for opportunities to serve your family and make their lives easier (and ask your children to do the same). Encourage your children to take care of the things that they have dominion over (their toys, rooms, homework, etc.), and make sure you are taking good care of the things that are in your dominion (keeping your house, grounds, finances, and car in order).

One word of caution, though: stewardship is not about keeping your things clean and well-maintained so that they can look like they belong in a museum; stewardship is *really* about keeping things clean and maintained so that others will feel comfortable using them. Yes, you must take care of the things you have been given, but if your family lives in fear of sitting on the couches, or even breathing on your precious car, or spending a penny of your hard-earned money, or if they miss you because you are so busy cleaning and classifying your collection of "ear plugs from around the world," you are offending stewardship because you are sending the message that things are more important than people. This affects sexuality, of course, because if your mate thinks that you value your things more than you value him or her, how can you reasonably expect your mate to offer the kind of trust that a whole and holy sexual relationship requires? Of course, you can't.

A good sense of self-discipline and true, hospitable stewardship in all the circumstances of one's life is essential to express a healthy, holy sexuality.

Faith

Faith is absolutely essential for a whole and holy sexuality because it clarifies what the ideal for Christian sexuality is, and provides a context for that sexuality to be expressed. The Vatican document *The Truth and Meaning of Human Sexuality* insists that any time we parents instruct or correct our children on sexual matters, we do so with the spiritual and moral dimensions of sexuality in mind. In fact, for the Christian, sexuality has its roots, not in biology, but in the soul. Sexuality is not merely the way one body expresses itself to another; it is really the way one soulful, mindful, noble, and embodied person expresses him- or herself to another soulful, mindful, noble, and embodied *person*. Likewise, the Christian is called to remember that the act of lovemaking is not merely an expression of love between a husband and wife, but rather, it is a physical metaphor for the intense, all-consuming passion with which God Himself seeks to love us (cf. the Song of Songs , or the Song of Solomon).

For the Christian, sexuality is really a prayer that enables us to give ourselves to work for the good of another as well as to bring unity and new life into the world. This is why even celibate priests and religious can have a vital sexuality, because sexuality is not so much a genital act as it is the act of using one's body and one's labors to bring about peace, to create new things, and to manifest God's passionate love for another.

In order to exhibit a sexuality that is founded on faith, we must first live out our faith in our everyday lives, and not be afraid to apply that faith to everything we do in the course of the day, including offering affection to our mate and children.

To that end, we must encourage our families to pray together, formally and informally, as well as to receive the sacraments frequently, and to engage in regular Bible reading and/or study. Beyond this, though, we must learn that prayer is not something that we do, but rather something that we are. Prayer does not simply consist of those things I do when I am in church or holding a rosary; it is also everything I do in the course of a day, from washing the dishes to doing my paperwork, to parenting my children, to making love with my mate, *if* I (*1*) seek to experience God in those moments and (*2*) seek to serve God in those moments.

Respect (1/2 cup self-respect with 1/2 cup respect for others)

This is a big one. Having a healthy respect for oneself and others includes such qualities as modesty, as well as the ability to treat others with the dignity they deserve, and the ability to set respectful limits when others accidentally or intentionally treat you in a manner that is beneath your God-given dignity. Applying respect to sexuality means that I have a good understanding of what it means to live and dress modestly (not dumpily, though; see below), I do not use others as a means to satisfy myself (either in or out of the bedroom), and I am good at setting limits with people who ask me to betray my God-given dignity. Let's take a look at each of these.

(a) Modesty

Though it involves such things, modesty has much more to do with one's internal attitude than it does with hemlines. The great Catholic physician and philosopher Dr. Herbert Ratner once said that a nun could be forced to walk naked down a street and still find a way to carry herself modestly, while Marilyn Monroe (or, perhaps a more contemporary example would be pop-singer Madonna) could walk down the street in a nun's full habit and still find a way to seem immodest.

Just as many people equate chastity with repression, many people equate modesty with dumpiness. A look at Church teaching on the matter shows that this is clearly not the case. As popular Catholic speaker Mary Beth Bonnacci wrote in an issue of *Envoy* magazine, certain people who think they are pursuing modesty ". . . seem to fear all attraction to the opposite sex. Some women seem to make a test out of requiring men to look past their deliberately slovenly appearance to find the 'gold' of inner beauty disguised within. Personally, I don't think this is such a hot idea."

She goes on to say, "The object of modesty is to elevate the dignity of the human person. It's to demonstrate that we respect the human body as the seat of the soul, as a gift from God. We keep the sexual function of the body private out of respect, but . . . we also show respect for our bodies when we dress attractively."

The upshot is that if we dress in a manner that glorifies ourselves, either by saying, "Look at what hot stuff I am" or, "Look at how piously dumpy I am," then we are being immodest.

Modesty is a social virtue that facilitates relationships by preventing people from behaving (or appearing) too shocking to each other, or behaving (or appearing) too fussily with each other. In order to practice and encourage modesty in your home, of course you should be sensitive to the message you and your children are sending by what you wear, but even more importantly, you should avoid gossiping about others to make yourself feel better, or more pious, more accomplished, and you should practice and encourage the ability to display all your gifts and talents while avoiding the temptation to say "Hey, everybody, LOOK AT ME!" all of the time.

(b) I do not use others to satisfy myself.

Using other people is an obvious affront to both respect and Christian sexuality. On the one hand, Christian sexuality calls us to be a generous, attentive, respectful, loving servant to another person. On the other hand, selfish sexuality causes us to think of ourselves as an itch that others are expected to scratch. But few people appreciate that selfishness in the bedroom has its roots far outside of the bedroom. For instance, as you go about your day: Do you shirk your responsibilities and expect everyone else to clean up your messes? Do you expect others to do for you what you are perfectly capable of doing for yourself? Do you attempt to act like your mate's superior, giving and denying permission for things that are important to him/her at will? Do you think about others primarily in terms of how associating with them can benefit you? If you said "yes," to any of the above, then chances are, whether you have intended to or not, you have made your mate feel used at one time or another, and I am willing to bet that you are experiencing the fallout from this "using" in your sexual relationship.

Discourage such selfish behavior in your own life and the lives of your children, and the generosity that takes its place will transfer to your and your children's sexuality as well.

(c) I am good at setting limits with people who ask me to betray my God-given dignity.

Setting respectful limits with others who either treat us in demeaning ways or ask us to do things that are beneath our God-given dignity is absolutely essential to developing solid character, to fostering healthy relationships, and to celebrating a healthy (and holy) sexuality.

If I do not know how to set limits, then I often feel taken advantage of by people who want me to do things that are really not good for me to do. The real problem, though, is not that others take advantage of me, but that I can't say "no" to people because I would feel too guilty disappointing them (or alternatively, too afraid of their anger). But my morality is dependent upon my ability to set limits, and my self-esteem is dependent upon how true I am to my morality. If we do not set respectful limits, we become like the Catholic woman I recently counseled whose husband regularly talked her into visiting strip clubs with him, as well as engaging in other immoral acts. As she put it, "I know it's wrong. I hate myself for doing it and I don't enjoy it at all, but he gets angry and accuses me of being 'holier than thou' when I try to say no, so I go just to try to keep the peace. After all, God wants us to have peaceful homes, right?"

Not at the expense of everything that is right, He doesn't!

If you wish to teach your children how to set respectful limits, I would recommend two things.

First, give them plenty of verbal and physical affection. Most people who do not set effective limits (especially around moral issues) do so because they were not appropriately affirmed as children. As adults, these individuals are so love-starved that they would do almost anything for approval, including violating everything they supposedly are and stand for. While this does not excuse their actions, it serves as a word to the wise for those parents wishing to raise children who are not morally spineless.

If you would like to become better at setting respectful limits in your life, then I would recommend *God Help Me, These People Are Driving Me Nuts! Making Peace with Difficult People* (Loyola, 2001).

Second, you need to teach your children to set respectful limits by giving them permission to respectfully tell you when they believe you are treating them disrespectfully. Now, I realize that there are some readers who will bristle at that comment. All I ask is that you hear me out before you decide that I am encouraging you to let your children undermine your parental authority. I am not. All I am suggesting is that in order to raise children who know how to respectfully stand up to others, you have to teach them what to say, and give them opportunities to say it, and chances are that the best time to teach this lesson is when you are unintentionally less than kind to your children.

Imagine the following scenario. You are running around the house trying to get ready for company. You see your son's room needs to be cleaned, but your son is playing video games instead of using the eyes God gave him to see that his room needs to be cleaned. True, you haven't asked him to clean his room yet, but even so. . . . Feeling frustrated and a little overwhelmed by all that needs to be done, you angrily say to your son, "Will you put that dumb game down and clean your room? We're trying to get ready for company here!"

Your son, because you have taught him well, does not yell at you. He doesn't even roll his eyes. What he does is look you in the eye and firmly but lovingly say, "Mom, that really hurt my feelings when you said that."

You think for a second and realize that, truth be told, you were not as respectful as you could have been, and so you say, "Look. I'm sorry. I shouldn't have yelled and called your game dumb. I'm just feeling a little overwhelmed, and I could use some help. Please, quickly finish your game and clean up."

Giving your child the right to respectfully challenge you when you are less than respectful yourself does not mean that you must let your child off the hook for doing what you ask. It does not even mean that you are giving your child permission to be rude to you. In fact, by teaching him exactly how and what it means to respectfully challenge you, you decrease the chances that your child will be hostile toward you at any time. Plus, by teaching your child that he/she has the right to stand up for him-/herself no matter who is demeaning him/her (unintentionally or not), you are teaching your child to have a moral backbone, which, in adulthood is critical if you want to have a healthy, holy sexuality.

Intimacy (combine equal parts verbal and emotional communication)

Intimacy, the ability to express yourself verbally and emotionally, is essential for both good character and a healthy sexuality because it is your large capacity for intimacy that helps other persons know where they stand at all times and prevents them from ever feeling used, because they know where you're coming from.

Intimacy is to love what a depth gauge is to a body of water. A couple — or for that matter a parent and child — may say that they love each other, but whether that love is a puddle or an ocean depends upon both persons' capacity for intimacy — that is, their capacity to express themselves verbally and emotionally.

There are some who believe that intimacy is gender-based in that it is a primarily "female" quality. For reasons that I will explain later (hint: it has to do with complementarity of roles and the original unity of man and woman), this concept flies in the face of Church teaching. For now, let it suffice to say that

---

You can find more tips on expanding your intimacy in *For Better . . . FOREVER! A Catholic Guide to Lifelong Marriage.*

Jesus Christ, who was fully human, fully man, and therefore fully masculine, was capable of deep intimacy with those He loved. Scripture shows convincingly that He was a man who was completely capable of expressing both His thoughts and His emotions very well. All men (and women) would do well to follow His example.

If you would like to foster more intimacy in your relationship, then challenge yourselves to spend time talking about your dreams for the future, your feelings about the present, as well as your feelings for each other. Men and women should both work to be as affectionate with each other as possible while retaining a sense of propriety. And husbands and wives should have at least a working knowledge of all the roles their mate plays and all the interests their mate has, so that they always have plenty to talk about.

To encourage your children's capacity for intimacy, again, affection is key, as is going out of your way to listen to them respectfully when they speak, and making sure to speak respectfully to them as well. Also, it is very important to give your children an emotional language. In other words, from their earliest years, ask them to tell you how they are feeling, and help them identify their feelings if they are struggling. If you ask your child how he feels and he says, "I don't know," say, "Well, you are walking around with your head down and your feet dragging on the ground and a sour look on your face. That usually means that someone is either sad or hurt. Which are you?"

Whether you guess correctly or not is beside the point. The real point is helping your children recognize their feelings and giving them the right words to speak about them. Of course it is just as important to teach them to listen to others who are sharing their thoughts or feelings. Intimacy is a two-way street. The child who knows this will grow up able to celebrate a truly godly, intimate relationship — able to offer the true intimacy (the sharing of self) that a healthy, holy sexuality requires.

Cooperation

Cooperation may seem like an odd virtue to include in a discussion on sexuality, but it is really quite important. Whether you are the sort of person who knows how to work respectfully with another to solve problems and meet goals is directly related to how well you are able to work with your spouse to create a mutually satisfying sexual relationship, plan the size of your family, negotiate the frequency of lovemaking, and make it through those times of continence that Natural Family Planning requires.

The best way to teach cooperation to your children is to show them how well you and your mate work together to resolve your conflicts and get things done around the home. Likewise, it is a good idea for the whole family to work and play together as much as possible so that the turn-taking, listening, respect, and goal-directed action that is required for good problem-solving are ever-present in their everyday lives.

Joy

Joy, as C.S. Lewis described it in his book *Surprised By Joy*, is really the ability to experience God in little events of daily living. It is the ability to look at a sunset, a tree, the face of a friend or the body of a lover and say, "God is so wonderful. Look at all the beauty he has surrounded me with."

Of course, Joy is the ability to celebrate the God-given pleasures of life. It is the virtue that the Jewish book of wisdom known as the *Caballah* speaks of when it says, "We will be held accountable before God for all the permitted pleasures which we fail to enjoy."

Some of you might wonder if joy is really a Catholic virtue; after all, we can be a pretty penitential lot sometimes. Even so, there is a season for everything, and there is room for both penance and joy in the Church. Even St. Francis, who was certainly good at doing without, was once asked, because Christmas that year fell on Friday (a fast day), if his brothers should fast or feast. His reply, "On such a day as Christmas, even the walls should be smeared with meat so that they could feast!"

Joy is an important part of our sexuality. It allows us to be playful with our mate, to laugh and be silly without taking or offering offense. It allows us to celebrate in each other's arms, and even to experience lovemaking as a physical metaphor for how passionately God Himself loves us. To encourage joy in our homes, parents must remember that they are never too old to play. Learn new things, have new experiences, and encourage your children to do the same. Play with your children, laugh with them, tell jokes, play games and make silly faces. And don't forget to thank God (and encourage your children to thank Him) for caring so much about you that He would permit you so many healthy pleasures in life.

Personhood

Personhood may sound like an odd characteristic, but it figures prominently in Pope John Paul II's writings. While it refers to many things, for our purposes, we are going to define it as encompassing three things:

1. An appreciation for what it means to be made in the image and likeness of God.
2. An acknowledgement of the goodness of the body and a respect for the spiritual meaning of the body.
3. An understanding of what it means to be a fully functioning Christian man or woman.

Whole books could be and have been written on these three things, and I cannot hope to do them justice in the short space I have available here. Nevertheless, we need to look at this quality at least briefly because it has everything to do with whether persons have a healthy and holy sense of their sexuality.

To appreciate being made in the image and likeness of God is to have an understanding of what it is to be a fully functioning human being. God is the source of our unique dignity because everything that we consider about ourselves to be good comes directly from God. As C.S. Lewis put it, "God lends us a little bit of his reason and that is how we think. He gives us his love and then holds our hand while we do it," like a little child learning to write his letters. Celebrating the fact that we are made in God's image and likeness means that each day we should try to increase our capacity, our facility, with all of the virtues that make us human. Every day, we look for opportunities to grow in love, creativity, intelligence, passion, joy, generosity, and all the virtues that enable us to live life as a gift. It is the ability to pursue these virtues, as well as our actual pursuit of these virtues, that makes us truly human.

So what does this have to do with sexuality? Everything. When I work to manifest the God-given virtues that underlie my humanity on a daily basis, I end up sanctifying my everyday life. Taking out the garbage is no longer about taking out the garbage; it becomes an opportunity for me to practice service or generosity. Likewise, when I truly understand what it is to be made in the image and likeness of God, lovemaking is not just a pleasant thing I do with my mate; it becomes an opportunity to practice all the virtues that make me human: self-donation, respect, temperance, joy, patience, a pro-life ethic, and so on. Personhood allows me to experience my sexuality as a prayer that elevates both my wife and me and manifests God's own love for each of us. To encourage this aspect of personhood, we need to acquaint ourselves and our children with the Works of Mercy (spiritual and corporal) as well as all the virtues we receive as a free and unmerited gift at Baptism — that is, the gifts and fruits of the Holy Spirit, the Cardinal virtues, and the Theological virtues. We need to encourage the development of these virtues in ourselves and our children in our everyday lives by looking for opportunities to live them out in the simple tasks we do, and through the family mission statement I discussed earlier. In this way, our children will understand that everything they do, think, and feel — even their sexuality — has a spiritual component and spiritual ramifications.

Regarding the second point, personhood is the quality that compels me to think of my body as a gift and to acknowledge my bodily functions not as "icky" but as an integral part of the creation God pronounces to be "good" in the Book of Genesis.

Recently, I counseled a woman who hated making love to her husband. By her own admission, her husband was a good and loving man; he was romantic and attentive, he did not demean her in any way, they did not have significant arguments, and, generally speaking, they were good friends. In other words, there was absolutely no relational justification for her lack of interest in lovemaking. So what was the problem? This woman was very uncomfortable with her body and bodily things. I asked her to write a journal entry on the topic of, "Describe what goes through your mind when you think about sex." This is an excerpt from that journal:

> "Sex. Ugh. I hate everything about it. I don't like being breathed on, I don't like being touched, especially on my private parts. After all, that's where I go to the bathroom from; why would I want to be touched there and why would I want to touch him there? How gross is that? And sex is so messy. I hate the squishy,

icky, mess of it all. I would be happy if I never had to have sex. Why can't my husband just get over his need for sex (I guess because he's a guy — that's what guys do, right?) and just concentrate on our spiritual lives?"

While the woman who wrote this was an otherwise fine person who had many positive qualities and traits, this kind of thinking (separating "spiritual things" from our bodily nature) represents a serious affront to the quality of personhood, and it is just the sort of dualism that has been condemned as heretical since the earliest days of Christianity. Personhood is the quality that allows us to understand the spiritual nature of material things, especially our bodies. To encourage the development of personhood in this context, we need to do two things. First, while being mindful of modesty, we need to not be "grossed out," shocked, or scandalized by our bodies and the things our bodies do. As Scripture says, "I give you thanks that I am fearfully, wonderfully made" (Ps 139:14, NAB). We must teach our children to be thankful for their bodies and all the things our bodies do, because all of those things were created by God to help our bodies function well. And God Himself pronounced them good. When people are struggling with this kind of loathing of their body and physical nature, counseling is almost always indicated, because such individuals are completely resistant to their spouses' encouragement to be more sexually forthcoming, because, to their minds the real problem is that their mate is simply "oversexed." While "oversexed" mates do exist, they are not as common as one might think.

Finally, personhood means having a proper understanding of what it is to be a man or a woman. Unfortunately, this is often the least understood concept, even by faithful Catholics.

Catholics and non-Catholics alike tend to give in to the line of thinking that says "men are from Mars and women are from Venus." They say things like, "Men are rational, sexual, competitive, logical, etc., and women are nurturing, communicative, romantic, emotional." While there truly are differences between the sexes, they are not so simple as all this.

The Church teaches that in the beginning, God shared the *same* aspects of Himself (i.e., the same sets of characteristics and virtues) with both male and female *human beings*. As John Paul II demonstrates in "The Original Unity of Men and Women," the fact that Adam said of Eve, "This at last is bone of my bones and flesh of my flesh" (Gen 2:23) dramatically shows that body, mind, and soul, Eve was a being to whom Adam could relate completely. Our First Parents were made of the same essential biological, psychological, emotional, and spiritual *stuff*.

At the dawn of creation, both men *and* women were given the ability to reason, emote, love, communicate, produce, set goals, nurture, and so on. Likewise, both men *and* women were called to live out *all* of these qualities to the fullest. However, based on how God created their bodies, Adam and Eve had different *styles* of applying these qualities to everyday life. So, for example, while both Adam and Eve were given the responsibility to nurture, emote, communicate, etc., God created Eve's body to *emphasize* such qualities in her life, and this emphasis was what God called "femininity." Likewise, while both Adam and Eve were given the responsibility to make plans, set goals, provide for their needs, solve problems, etc., God created Adam's body to *emphasize* such qualities in his life, and this emphasis is what the Lord called "masculinity."

A good example of these emphases at work is how men and women practice their call to nurture young children. God ordained a woman's body to nurse her young. But even though men cannot lactate, God still requires them to be abundantly present and active in the lives of their children, just as God, Our Father, is present and active in our lives. God gave both men and women the ability to be *fully* nurturing and loving, but He ordained the sexes to express this fullness in equally valuable, yet different and complementary ways. As John Paul II taught us, men and women must prayerfully contemplate and emphasize their *bodies' unique capabilities* in order to first understand true masculinity and femininity. Then, we must use our masculinity and femininity as the prism through which we express our *full humanity*.

In trying to model and teach our children what it is to be a man or woman of God, we would do well to avoid the attitudes that say things like, "Women shouldn't handle the finances because that's a man's job" and "Men aren't good at nurturing children because that's a woman's job." It is exactly this attitude that offends the generosity required of a sacramental marriage (by limiting the ways a husband and wife are willing to serve each other) and flies in the face of what the Church says God originally intended when he created men and women.

If we want to teach our children the true meaning of masculinity and femininity, we must avoid the use of limited templates that offer too narrow a definition of manliness or womanliness (like, "All men are athletic; all women like to decorate") and instead encourage our children to exhibit all of the qualities God has given them to the fullest throughout the bodies that God has given them. We should allow our boys to work alongside their fathers as they seek to live out all of the God-given virtues in their everyday lives. We should allow our girls to work alongside their mothers as they seek to live out all of the qualities that make them human through the bodies that God has given them. In this way, our children will learn that men and women are capable of many of the same things, but they will approach these tasks with a slightly different perspective and use slightly different methods. Even so, each has equal dignity in the eyes of the Lord and each brings unique gifts to every task they work on together, or independently.

So, There You Have It

Throughout this chapter, I have attempted to broaden your understanding of what it means to teach your kids to have a healthy, holy sexuality. As you have seen, sexuality is about so much more than "how we use and keep custody of our genitals." Rather, sexuality is ultimately about how we communicate ourselves to others and use our bodies to work for the good of others, whether that is on a one-on-one basis in marriage or in the broader, more spiritual sense of serving the world through celibate and religious life.

Now that we have dealt with sexuality in the broadest sense, I am going to begin zeroing in on what it takes to teach your children about the genital/sexual aspects of their sexuality. Most importantly, we are going to examine what it takes to do this with confidence, gentleness, and faith.

CHAPTER TWO

Getting Out of Your Own Way

Preparing to Talk to Your Kids About Sex

Erica and Marcus were serious Catholics who had both remained virgins until marriage. While they both expected their sex lives to take off after saying "I do," they found that somehow the marriage license didn't turn out to be the permission slip they thought it would be.

As Marcus explained, "It took a lot for Erica and me to remain virgins until we were married. We both had plenty of opportunities to have sex with other people before we met each other, and we certainly had ample opportunities to sleep together when we were dating. Worse, most of my friends were always talking about their conquests and calling me "gay" because I wasn't "getting any." Erica's friends in her sorority weren't much better, from what she tells me. But through all of that, we managed to save ourselves until marriage. Sad to say, though, the mental walls we built to keep ourselves sexually inactive all those years weren't so easy to take down, even once we were married."

Erica and Marcus found themselves arguing about their sexual relationship almost from the beginning. They disagreed about frequency. (Erica laughed, "I know it's supposed to be the other way around, but I think I wanted to make love even more often than he did.") They argued over whether certain sexual positions were "degrading" or not, whether certain acts (like oral sex as part of foreplay) were moral or not, and many other issues.

Erica continued, "It was tough to work all of that out after we were married. We had a great friendship, but in spite of (or maybe because of) all our abstinence training, nobody ever really taught us how to have a really satisfying marital sexuality. We had to work all that out for ourselves."

Even though Erica and Marcus both agree that by their tenth anniversary they had gotten to the point where they both had a vital and mutually satisfying sexual relationship, they wondered if there is a way to encourage their children to remain sexually pure until marriage, without having them go through a similar, painful period of trial and error in their own married lives.

Celia and Luke wanted to be able to teach their children how to have a healthy and holy sexuality, but in spite of themselves they felt uncomfortable about the topic. Their own sexual histories as single people were less than stellar, although they had been faithful to each other since marriage and tried hard to follow Church teaching on sexual ethics once they were married. On the one hand, they wanted to teach their children the importance of waiting until marriage to engage in sex, but, as Celia put it, "We have some nerve to hold our children to a standard that we weren't able to live up to ourselves. I mean, I want to do it, but I'm not sure how to do it without feeling like some kind of hypocrite."

When it comes to having healthy, age-appropriate conversations with their kids about sex, there are two major obstacles that stand between parents and their children: first, the awkwardness and confusion parents feel in addressing the subject at all, much less trying to integrate their faith with the lessons their children need to have a rewarding marital sex life; and second, the guilt they may be experiencing over their own sexual histories. In this chapter, it is my hope to help you overcome some of that awkwardness, whether it is due to simple confusion over what to tell your children or whether it is due to your feelings that, considering your own sexual history, you are less than a credible witness to what a healthy, Christian, sexuality is all about.

Catholic Sexuality: a Creature Set Apart

I believe that the most important thing to keep in mind when thinking and talking about Catholic sexuality is that it is a completely different — and ultimately superior — thing to every other form of sexuality that exists on the planet. Period. When we are preparing to talk to our children about sex, it is not enough to try to explain why Christians think *differently* about sexuality than the rest of the world does. Such approaches end up inadvertently sounding as if the secular approaches to sex are infinitely more rewarding, except that Christians are more "disciplined" about their sexuality, which of course, sounds like great fun to the average fourteen-year-old. Rather, I would suggest taking an approach that suggests that what the pagans do isn't really even true sexuality (often, to be perfectly blunt, it is merely eroticism and/or masturbation with another person present). Yes, the two things (i.e., what the pagans do versus what true sexuality is really about) look similar on the surface, but they are still totally different, because the true Christian version of sexuality is what God intended when He gave us sexuality in the first place. It is infinitely more real, beautiful, and satisfying than the shabby imitations the world attempts to foist on us. Let me try to explain.

Imagine that you wanted to plant a flower garden. Now, you have two options available to you. You can either use plastic (or even silk) flowers, or you could use real flowers. At first thought, you might be leaning toward the artificial flowers because you might think of all the benefits artificial flowers give. For example, you would get instant gratification by being able to see what your garden will look like. You wouldn't have to water or fertilize, animals wouldn't eat your flora, and you would never have to trim your plants or transplant. It would be great, right? Well, maybe. After all, while artificial flowers might look good at first — from a distance — they look pretty tacky on closer examination, especially sticking up out of the dirt where they look downright ridiculous. Furthermore, artificial plants get dirty when it rains and will fade in the sun, and they don't grow back when you accidentally hack them up with the weed-whacker. Last but not least, even the most expertly made artificial flowers don't smell like anything. Of course, you could rectify this by spraying your favorite cologne or *parfum* all over them, but imagine your embarrassment at trying to explain to your friends why your alleged "rose bushes" smell oddly like *Big Musky Man* or *L'eau de Sexpot*.

So — and not a moment too soon — you begin to consider the second option. Real flowers. Yes, there is more work involved. You have to water and fertilize, and you have to keep the local rodents from lining up for the floral buffet, and you have to trim and trellis, and occasionally transplant. But they do not fade with time; in fact, they become more beautiful. They bear up under close scrutiny. Unlike the tacky plastic flowers, real flowers actually become more delightful when you look at them closely. They are constantly changing and growing and becoming more alluring, continually bursting forth with new life and new color. Likewise, few things are more wonderful than coming home at the end of a long day and being enveloped by the delicious fragrance of lavender, roses, freesia, lemon grass, and hundreds of other kinds of real flowers.

In the same way, what passes for secular, pagan "sexuality" is merely a shabby, tacky imitation of what sex really is. They don't have the real thing; *we do*. Honestly, most of secular society can't handle the truth, and so they try to come up with some tacky, plastic-covered (often literally speaking) approximation of what sex is supposed to be, and then offer it up to the rest of the world as the best kind of sexuality, just like the plastic flowers in our analogy. But on closer examination, their version of sex doesn't hold up. It isn't vital, because it is openly hostile to new life, and rather than flowing from a deep spiritual friendship between two people, it seeks to replace and subvert that friendship. It doesn't improve with time (in fact, it fades) because no real intimacy can exist in the absence of a spiritual friendship, and without intimacy, lovemaking of any kind becomes boring and less interesting with time. And it doesn't stand up to conflict and stress (the weed-whacker in the metaphor) because, in the secular version of sexuality, there isn't supposed to be conflict and stress, only blissful ecstasy, and so at the first signs of trouble, the passion dies and the couple breaks apart.

Catholic sexuality, on the other hand, offers something completely different. It offers the chance to never feel used by someone. It offers the freedom to be playful and joyful with someone in a way that is never demeaning or degrading. It allows a couple to experience their lovemaking as a physical metaphor for the passion God Himself has for the couple. It allows a couple to communicate their whole physical, emotional, spiritual, and relational selves with each other every time they make love. It invites the couple to physically restate their wedding vows — and celebrate a sacrament — every time they make love. It offers protection from disease and heartbreak. It encourages the couple to celebrate a love so powerful, so profound, that in nine months, that love has to be given its own name. It encourages a couple to prayerfully consider God's plan for their lives every month, and ask whether in that month God is calling them to strengthen the bonds that already exist, or to expand the "community of love" that is the family by adding another life to the family. It challenges our capacity for vulnerability and helps us overcome the basic shame that all humanity experienced after the fall in the Garden of Eden, and so it plays a part in preparing us to stand, completely exposed, before our Divine Lover when we arrive for the eternal wedding feast with God. And so much more.

In short, the comparison between Catholic sexuality and the eroticism secular society serves up and has the audacity to call "sexuality" is like comparing real flowers to fake ones. There is no comparison.

This mindset serves three functions. First, if we, as parents, do not experience Catholic sexuality as the joyful, fulfilling, life-giving, spiritual, and profoundly beautiful reality that it is, then we need to get our own sexual attitudes in order because we cannot give to our children what we ourselves do not have.

The second thing this mindset does is take away the pressure to compete in any way with what the secular world has to offer. When we talk to our children about sex, we can freely admit what seemingly attractive, ultimately shabby things the world has to offer, but then immediately point to how *superior* Catholic sexuality is, not just in a spiritual sense but in the physical, emotional, and relational departments as well. For example, we can freely admit that the world says, "Enjoy yourself! Have sex with whomever you want, whenever you want. Pleasure yourself, and

If you are looking for resources to help you do this, my marriage book, *For Better . . . FOREVER!* is a good place to start.

when you are done with your lovers, throw them away." Then we can go on to point out the fact that this attitude is so much inferior to the Catholic attitude that says, "Of course you must enjoy your sexuality. So, in order to do that, make sure you find a partner who can love you as passionately, respectfully, powerfully, and prayerfully as God Himself wants you to be loved. Find someone who thinks, speaks, and acts as if you are their greatest treasure, save only their Faith and their breath, and then hold on to that person for the rest of your life as your greatest treasure next to Jesus Christ and your own life. Find a lover who wants to help you become the person God created you to be, who looks at you and sees his or her unborn children in your eyes, who knows how to control him- or herself so that you never feel used or threatened and so can give yourself totally. Find someone who encourages you in all the things you want to do and all the things God is calling you to be."

From this point, you can go on to say that, yes, true sexuality (as opposed to the dross that secular society holds up) is harder to attain. It involves some discipline, some work, some self-control, but it is also the only kind of sexuality in which your children can hope to find true joy, true divine love, true fulfillment, true trust, and true vitality. Anything else is foolishness, pain, and possibly death.

The Golden Cow Chip

Let me suggest an object lesson that will help you set this up for your child. The very first time you are going to talk to your child about sex, do this first. Spray paint a "cow chip" (or rock — just pretend that it is a cow chip) with bright gold paint. Then, take an amount of money that your child would say was significant (you decide how much that is, or how much you can afford) and put it in a paper bag (separate from the cow chip of course, which can stand all on its own). Sit your child down and say, "I want to give you something, but you'll have to make a choice. First, I have this beautiful golden cow chip." Show the lump, describe how beautiful it is — don't be afraid to sound ridiculous. Talk about all the advantages of the lump (it's a good paperweight, it's good for throwing at people you are angry with, plus it is the most beautiful fertilizer anyone could ever want), and how nice it would look sitting on your child's shelf. Then, casually mention that, "Oh, yes, I also have this bag of money (state the amount) *which I will give you* if you really want it. But it really isn't nearly as pretty as the golden lump."

If your child has half a brain, after you convince your child that you are really serious about giving him or her the cash, he or she will probably go for the money. But before you give it your child, say, "Well, if you *really* want it, of course you can have it. But first you would have to do some work (of course, you could have the cow chip for free)."

When your child says, "What kind of work?" describe a task that is significantly harder than what you might normally ask him or her to do, but not so hard that he or she would find it impossible or disheartening (or not worth the money you are paying), and offer to pay your child the money in the bag for completing the task. "Or," you say with a smile, "you can have this golden cow chip right now."

Of course, your child will think you are an idiot for this little demonstration, but since this won't be the first or last time your child feels this way about you, don't let on what your real purpose is. Just let him/her make the choice, do the work, sweat and struggle, then collect the cash. After you award your child the money in the bag, then you are ready to have your talk about sex.

You: *You know how I asked you to make that really stupid choice between the money and the golden cow chip? And how, even though it was harder, you chose to do the work to win the money?*

Child: *Yeah?*

You: *Well, you are at an age when pretty soon you are going to have to make another choice just like it . . . .*

You can then talk about how the world offers up a "golden cow chip" in the form of eroticism, selfishness, sex with whomever, whenever you choose, that looks good on the outside but inside is empty, useless, and frankly stinks, causing anyone who touches it to stink as well. Because it looks so good on the outside, many people choose it, and just as many people realize too late, after the real prize is lost, that they have chosen badly — that their choice has led to heartbreak, loneliness, depression, disease, or even death. Of course, God can always take away the stink that comes from having touched the "golden cow chip," but having touched it, any time that person sees *anything* golden, even real gold, they will remember that smell first, and feel a little sick inside from the memory. In fact, even though God can take away the stink, some people feel so sick from the memory of that smell, that they may never be able to enjoy real gold again.

Then you can explain that, just as your child *wisely* chose the bag of money even though it involved more work, you are going to ask your child to choose true sexuality, Catholic sexuality, which is so much more wonderful, enjoyable, and rewarding than anything the world has to offer that you actually have to work hard to win it. Just as your child had to work — hard — to win the money. Ask your child if he or she is glad of the choice to work to win the money. Then ask your child which he/she would rather have: a truly rewarding, joyful, Catholic sexuality, or the "golden cow chip the world has to offer." Once your child makes his or her next wise choice, take the next several years consistently teaching what the prize is, and how to succeed at the work it takes to win the prize.

Of course, the point to all this is that many Christians feel almost apologetic trying to explain Catholic sexuality to their children. "Yes, dear, those people in the world are sure having a lot of fun. But we're Christians, and Christians aren't allowed to have fun." This is entirely the wrong attitude. Because of our Christianity, we are actually empowered to have a more rewarding sexuality than any other group of people. This is borne out time and again by studies reporting that religious married couples make love more often, and find their sexual relationships more satisfying, than their secular counterparts. How could this be unless Christian sexuality was really something altogether superior to what the world has to offer — and not just on some nebulous (albeit important) spiritual level either?

Erica and Marcus, the couple whose story began this chapter, were concerned about how to teach their children to save themselves for marriage on the one hand, and on the other hand how not to deal with the same issues of awkwardness and repression that they experienced in the early years of their marriage. Teaching your children to have the attitude that I am describing here prevents this problem. How? Because the classic way to talk to kids about sex (the way both Marcus and Erica were trained) is to say that sex is forbidden (even poisoned) fruit which is not safe to eat until marriage. This view often creates people who may successfully avoid sexual sins before marriage, but who then are left with a viscerally negative reaction to sex, even though they find the idea of having a rewarding marital intimacy intellectually appealing. But by adopting the new attitude I am describing in these pages, you are not teaching your children that sex is forbidden, poisoned fruit until marriage. Rather, you are teaching them that sex is a beautiful fruit *that simply does not ripen until marriage*. You *could* eat it sooner, but it would not be as sweet, it wouldn't be as fulfilling, and worse, it could make you sick in heart and body and very well spoil your appetite for the fruit when it finally did ripen. And that really would be a tragedy. Allow me to offer one more story to illustrate this point.

There is a wonderful part of C.S. Lewis's book *The Magician's Nephew* in which a golden apple tree (the tree from which the wardrobe in *The Lion, the Witch, and the Wardrobe* is later made) is planted to keep the evil witch out of Narnia for a long, long time. While the tree is growing, though, the witch sneaks in, steals an apple, and gleefully eats it. The child heroine in the story is confused as to how this tree can really keep the witch out, since she didn't seem to mind eating its fruits presently. The child puts her question to the great lion, Aslan.

> ". . . Aslan," she said, ". . . there must be some mistake, . . . [the Witch] can't really mind the smell of those [magical, golden] apples. . . . she ate one."
>
> "Child," he replied, "that is why all the rest are now a horror to her. That is what happens to those who pluck and eat fruits at the wrong time and in the wrong way. The fruit is good, but they loathe it ever after."
>
> — C.S. Lewis,
> *The Magician's Nephew*

And so it is with sex. While I do not mean to suggest that Lewis was writing about sexuality, the metaphor applies here anyway. We should not teach our children to fear the forbidden fruit of sex until they say their vows — which in this version of the story become some kind of antidote that will allow them to choke down the poisoned apple. Rather, we must teach our children that *true sexuality is the golden apple*, which is more delicious, more magical, more fulfilling than any other apple in the garden, *but it must be plucked and eaten at the right time* in order for us to experience its full goodness. A person *could* choose to eat it sooner, when it is not ripe; unfortunately he or she would run the risk of finding the fruit sweet to the lips but hard on the stomach. And because of this, he or she would come to loathe it ever after.

The Third Thing

As I mentioned earlier, there is a third benefit to adopting this attitude — that Christian sexuality is so superior to every other form of "sexuality" that it is, in fact, an entirely different thing (that is, it is the *real* thing). That third benefit is this. It eliminates the awkwardness you may feel in holding your children to a sexual standard that you yourself may not have upheld in your own adolescence or young adulthood. At the beginning of this chapter you read the story of Celia and Luke, who had not remained virgins until marriage. Though they wanted to teach their children the truth of the Church, they also struggled with feeling like hypocrites for holding their children to a different standard than they held themselves to in their earlier years.

Of course, this attitude, however understandable, does not make sense on several levels. For example, if you were poor, uneducated, or deprived in some way as an adolescent or young adult, you would not want your children to grow up to live the same level of poverty, ignorance, or deprivation, would you? Of course not. You would hold them to a higher standard. You would give them the tools to do better than you did, and you would require them to use those tools to achieve a more fulfilling, satisfying life. Moreover, you would not feel like a hypocrite for having held them to a higher standard; you would feel proud. So why would you not feel the same way about giving your children the tools they needed to live out a truly rewarding, joyful, chaste, Catholic sexuality, require them to use those tools, and feel proud of yourself for having done better by your children than was done for you?

Here's why. Because hidden in the comment that "we don't want to hold our children to a higher sexual standard than we held" is the notion that Catholic sexuality is something that people gravitate toward after they have had their fun and are now ready to settle down and get serious about life. In other words, this comment hides the belief that Catholic sexuality is better for the soul but not nearly as enjoyable.

In my opinion, the person who feels this way about Catholic sexuality (real sex) is dealing with one, or some combination, of two problems. Either this person really doesn't understand what true Catholic sexuality is all about, or (s)he is experiencing a case of the golden apple having been eaten at the wrong time (and therefore tends to think of Catholic sexuality in a somewhat penitential light).

By contrast, the couple who, though having had a less-than-saintly past, have both educated themselves about the truth of Catholic sexuality and worked through their own sexual baggage, see that their own previous sexual experiences actually served as an obstacle to the joyful, life-giving, soulful, intimate, respectful, passionate, spiritual sexuality that the Church encourages them to celebrate. Because these couples are happier now than they have ever been in their sexual lives, they can actually say to their children, *"I know what you are going to go through in adolescence and young adulthood, and I want to tell you something. I thought that sleeping with someone before marriage (and whatever else you thought) was going to be a wonderful thing. And at the time, I did think it was pretty good. But I had no idea what I was missing by not saving myself for marriage, and because I didn't save myself, your mom (dad) and I had to work through a lot of painful stuff [N.B.: no need to be more specific here unless you feel certain details would be proper and important to share] to get to the great place where we are today. And then, when we finally got to the place where we worked through our struggles, we realized that this is what the Church wanted us to have all along and we could have saved ourselves so much pain and so many arguments if we had just chosen to listen to what the Church and our parents told us in the first place.*

"I know you are going to have to make your own choices, just like I did. But I really hope you choose better than I did, not just because 'the Church says so' or I want you to, but because the early years of your life and marriage will be so much better than mine were if you do. I just wanted to tell you that because I love you, and I trust you to do even better than me in your life."

You may think that this is wishful thinking, but I recently had a woman tell me about a talk she had with her son that was very much like the one I described above, except for one thing. She and her husband did not have a fulfilling, Catholic sexuality. In fact, they were getting divorced — in large part because the husband had had a series of affairs and struggled with sexual addictions all his life.

She told me that although her son did not know the details, he knew that his father had slept around before marriage (he had said so) and he also knew that his dad had cheated on his mother. On one occasion, when she and her son were discussing sex and her wish that he would save himself for marriage, she told him, *"I love your dad very much even now. And we both always wanted to work through our problems and stay together. But when you sleep with somebody, you give a part of yourself away, and the more people you have sex with, the more of yourself you give away; even if you don't mean to, it still happens because that's how sex works. Sometimes, you can give so much of yourself away that there isn't enough of you left to be able to solve the problems in your life and your marriage — and you just get lost. That's what happened to your dad and me. I don't ever want you to have to go through that. That's why I hope you will save yourself for marriage."*

Celebrating a Healthy, Catholic Sexuality in Your Own Marriage

Whether you identify more with the couple who have worked through their sexual baggage and educated themselves on what true Catholic sexuality is supposed to be, or you identify more with the woman whose marital situation was far from ideal, it will be important for you to have a good working knowledge of what Catholic sexuality is really supposed to be about, because as the quote above suggests, your own attitudes and relationship with your mate will be the most influential teacher your children ever encounter.

Why Catholics Do It Infallibly

The Four Paths of Sacred Sex

1. Catholics are Called to Approach Lovemaking Joyfully.

Catholics are encouraged to celebrate the sacraments frequently and joyfully. Marriage is one sacrament I hope you will not give me too much trouble about celebrating in such a way. Sex is not a duty, a chore, an extra, or even a "nice thing" to do when you have the energy. If you are married, then lovemaking is the foundation of your vocation. It is God's first commandment to all of humanity. (When God said, "Be fruitful and multiply" [Gen 1:28]), He wasn't giving math homework.)

The first obstacle most couples encounter to experiencing the joy the Church encourages them to is that they simply don't understand the importance of lovemaking as the primary joy and "work" of marriage. Too many married couples think of sex as just another thing to do — albeit a pleasant-enough thing — at the end of a long, exhausting day. With such an attitude, it is no wonder that Inhibited Sexual Desire Disorder (i.e., the lack of sexual desire between a husband and wife, which is most often due to a devaluation of the spiritual and psychological dimensions of sexuality) is one of the most prevalent psychological and relationship problems in Western Society. Christians who both use NFP and take the vocation of marriage seriously rarely fall prey to this disorder because they understand that lovemaking represents a physical re-enactment of their wedding vows and wedding day. I don't know about you, but I was exhausted on my wedding day, and so was my wife. All those months of wedding preparations had, frankly, taken their toll. Even so, it would never have occurred to either of us to call the pastor the morning of the ceremony and say, "You know Father, we were thinking we should just put this marriage thing off until we're a little less tired and stressed. Maybe next week sometime; we'll let you know."

On the contrary, as exhausted as we were, somehow we actually drew strength from the wedding ceremony and the celebration that followed. In the same way, couples who understand that lovemaking is a re-enactment of their wedding day never take their sexuality for granted. They tend to put as much energy into planning and keeping their romantic life vital and satisfying as they did preparing their original wedding celebration. And they draw as much strength from their sexual relationship as they did the first day they said "I do" to each other.

A second major obstacle to a joyful sexuality is that too many Christian husbands and wives confuse modesty with shame and awkwardness about their sexuality. While modesty "protects the intimate center of the person" (*Catechism of the Catholic Church, #2521*) and prevents us from being reduced to sexual objects, modesty also "authorizes sexual display where genial fulfillment is allowed, that is, in marriage" (*Encyclopedia of Catholic Doctrine*).

Shame, on the other hand, causes us to hold back just where we are called to be generous. It prevents sex from being the "self-gift" the Holy Father says it ought to be. Our sexual and bodily shame is a direct descendent of the shame Adam and Eve encountered after the Fall, standing before God in their nakedness (Genesis teaches that Adam and Eve became ashamed of their nakedness only after the Fall, a nakedness which the Holy Father teaches — and any discerning reader should be able to tell — goes far beyond mere physical nudity (cf. Pope John Paul II's *The Original Unity of Man and Woman: A Catechesis on the Book of Genesis*). If we are ashamed of being exposed and vulnerable before a mate — be that physically, emotionally, spiritually, or psychologically — how will we ever tolerate standing exposed and vulnerable before our Divine Lover? By challenging our fears of vulnerability and overcoming our resistance to "losing control," we may learn to find joy, not only in the arms of our earthly lover, but in the presence of our Heavenly Lover as well.

2. Maintain a Responsible Openness to Life.

For sexuality to be truly spiritual, we must learn to balance the virtues expressed by what the Church calls "responsible parenthood." What's that? you ask. Basically, it boils down to this.

On the one hand,

Marriage and conjugal love are by their nature ordained toward the begetting and educating of children. Children are really the supreme gift of marriage and contribute very substantially to the well-being of their parents. . . . Hence, while not making the other purposes of matrimony of less account, . . . the couple . . . should regard as their proper mission the task of transmitting human life and educating those to whom it has been transmitted [that is, the children already born].

Gaudium et Spes #50a

On the other hand,

. . . while a child is a great blessing, it is sometimes very important for parents to give careful thought to the size of their families. Husband and wife "will thoroughly take into account both their own welfare and that of their children, those already born and those which may be foreseen. For this accounting they will reckon with both the material and the spiritual conditions of the times as well as their state of life. Finally, they will consult the interests of the family group, of temporal society, and of the Church herself. The married partners themselves should make this judgment, in the sight of God.

The Teaching of Christ and *Gaudium et Spes* # 50b

As is suggested by these two quotes from *Gaudium et Spes*, as well as the Church's teaching on marriage as a whole, responsible parenthood necessitates *finding the balance* between the unitive and procreative ends of marriage. Each of these "ends" (i.e., "goals" or "purposes") of marriage represent two distinct but equally important sets of virtues in the Christian life. For example, the unitive end of marriage emphasizes the couple's responsibility to manifest the same passion, intimacy, unity, fidelity, self-discipline, understanding, self-donation, etc., that Christ Himself shares in His relationship with the whole Church. Thanks to the unitive end of marriage, we should be able to point to any sacramentally married couple and say, "Jesus Christ loves me as intensely, faithfully, and passionately as they love each other." Likewise, while there is some overlap, the procreative end of marriage emphasizes a different set of virtues. The couple who lives out the procreative end of marriage to the fullest is a powerful witness to the virtues of community, generosity, solidarity, selflessness, paternity/maternity, trust in God's providence, and so on. Thanks to the procreative end of marriage, we should be able to look at any sacramentally married couple and say, "God gives Himself to me and all of His creation as generously as that couple give themselves to each other, to the children they have, and to the children they are planning to have."

Balancing and perfecting these two ends of marriage is a sanctifying work for the husband and wife, and it offers a powerful witness of God's love to the world. Could anyone claim to be a good Christian while intentionally ignoring one set of these virtues or the other? Of course not. And so the Church proscribes responsible parenthood, and offers Natural Family Planning, as a means of not only planning family size, but also of perfecting and confirming each husband and wife in *all* the virtues which are an essential part of the Christian walk. In *Christifidelis Laici*, the Holy Father tells us that the human family is modeled after the Trinity Itself. In fact, the Holy Father tells us that God, in His most basic nature as Trinity, is a family. In the "family" that is the Trinity, there is a perfect balance between unity and creativity. The Trinity loves each other so much (unity), that it almost cannot help but bring more life into the world with whom to share that love (creativity). Then, by sharing that love, the Trinity actually celebrates even greater unity, as that creation is drawn up more and more into the life of the Trinity.

The husband and wife seeking to model themselves after the Trinity do not have children merely out of a sense of duty or obligation, or to save a troubled relationship, or because the neighbors will think badly of them if they don't. After all, the Trinity does not create for any of these reasons. Similarly, the family modeling themselves after the Trinity does not have children for merely romantic reasons while failing to give serious consideration to being able to meet the needs of those children. After all, the Trinity makes certain it is capable of meeting the needs of all the children created through its love. Instead, the husband and wife modeling themselves after the Trinity bring life into the world for no other reason than to witness to the fact that, in their daily life together, they celebrate a divinely inspired love and intimacy so profound; a communion so powerful that — as Dr. Scott Hahn has put it — "in nine months it has to be given its own name." Celebrating responsible parenthood in your marriage gives you the tools you need, not only to help you decide how many children to have, but also to build and foster this kind of godly, creative, self-donative love in your marriage as a whole.

From time to time, I have heard faithful Catholics comment that the "default" in marriage is "set" to having children. In fact, while we must always leave our hearts open to the possibility of children, the "default" in marriage is not set to either having or not having children. The "default" is set to "prayer." As *Gaudium et Spes* says, "The married partners themselves should make this judgment [regarding whether or not to conceive at any given time] in the sight of God." To help us become more like the Trinity which we are called to image, God will, at various times call us to conceive, or postpone a pregnancy. For example, in some months, through prayerful consideration of their "state of life" (cf. GS #50 above), a couple may be led by God to postpone conception and instead work on the unitive goals of their marriage, so that they can nurture the love and intimacy God desires them to share, and to foster the community between and among the children He has already given them. In other months, through prayerful consideration of their state of life, God will lead a couple to add another member to their "community of love" (the family) which will in turn give all concerned greater opportunities to practice unity and self-donative love. Through NFP, the unitive and procreative ends of marriage can be celebrated as a joyful, ever-expanding circle of love through which each family member is aided by the grace of marriage to become "perfect as your heavenly Father is perfect" (Mt 5:48).

Each month, I encourage you and your mate to practice the second path to sacred sexuality — responsible parenthood. I encourage you to use the gift of NFP to prayerfully consider the state of your life and marriage and to discern which end of marriage God is calling you to emphasize at this time in your lives. Is God, through the circumstances of your life, asking you to concentrate on nurturing the community of love that is your family? Is He asking you to take advantage of some "creative continence" time this month either to get your priorities in order or to learn how to better meet each other's needs, or to build up the intimacy, generous service, respect, passion, and self-donative love that empowers you to image the union experienced by the Trinity? Or, alternatively, is God calling you to celebrate and expand the community of love you already have by adding a new life to your family? Only you can decide which of these two ends of marriage God is asking you to concentrate on this month, and you can decide this only by standing with your mate in the presence of God and asking Him to give you a greater heart for love as well as the wisdom needed to be good stewards of the lives and love He is already sharing with you.

3. Approach Each Other in Prayer.

Some people sniff at the notion of joining prayer and lovemaking as if it serves the same function as reciting baseball statistics. But prayer is absolutely essential to a spiritual sexuality. Mine goes something like this, *"Lord, let me kiss her with your lips, love her with your gentle hands, consume her with your undying passion that I may show her how precious and beautiful she is to us."* Develop your own "lover's prayer" and see if the Lord doesn't help you become a more generous, loving, and attentive partner.

4. Guard Each Other's Dignity.

The virtues I have mentioned, especially vulnerability, cannot flourish except in a marriage where the couple are fierce guardians of each other's dignity. Spiritual sexuality cannot exist in the face of cruel humor, blunt criticism, name-calling, neglect, abuse, or other affronts to one's personal dignity. The most definitive research on marriage tells us that for a couple to be happy there must be *five times* more affection, generosity, and kindness, than criticism, nagging, arguing, or expressions of contempt. Moreover, it has been my experience that this 5:1 ratio is only the beginning point of spiritual sexuality. If a couple exhibit a solid, sacred sexuality, then it is more likely that their positivity to negativity ratio is 7:1, or even 10:1.

If you want to achieve a true Catholic sexuality, then the only answer is to love. Love more, love better, love every day.

Not necessarily because your spouse deserves it, but because your Christian dignity demands it.

Some Final Thoughts

In the course of this chapter, it has been my attempt to show you how Catholic sexuality, rather than being the "poor, older, more shriveled up and settled-down cousin" to secular sexuality, is actually much more wonderful than anything the world could dream up. In fact, secular "sexuality" is really just a cheap imitation of the real thing, which is the life-giving, soul-uniting, passionate, joyful, deeply spiritual, and profoundly fulfilling kind of sexuality the Church encourages her couples to celebrate.

When you understand what Catholic sexuality is really about, it allows you to be confident presenting it to your children, regardless of your own history, because you understand that you are offering the best to your child — not just spiritually speaking, but emotionally, psychologically, and relationally as well.

Finally, because the model you present to your own children is so important, I would encourage you to educate yourselves further about the whole truth regarding Catholic sexuality. Sort through your own sexual baggage and resolve the sexual concerns/disagreements that may interfere with celebrating a truly joyful, life-giving, unifying, passionate, Catholic sexuality in your marriage.

Now that we have reviewed many of the things you need to know in order to approach the sexual education of your children from a healthy, faith-filled perspective, the next chapter is going to get down to business, as we discover the specifics of talking to your kids about sex.

CHAPTER THREE

R-E-S-P-E-C-T!

Talking the Talk

In part two of this book, we are going to explore the different stages of your child's development and offer specific suggestions for fostering his or her sexuality and character (by now, I hope you understand that for the Christian these two are inextricably tied to each other). But before we visit those stages, it will be important to review the seven principles for having healthy age-appropriate conversations with your children. Represented by the acronym RESPECT, the seven principles are as follows:

Realize what they need to know and when.
Elicit your child's thoughts, attitudes, and feelings.
Speak the truth.
Present a positive, Christian attitude toward sex.
Expect to talk about your own struggles when appropriate.
Control your temper and the temptation to lecture.
Teach your child what the gift of the body is for.

Let's take a look at each of the above:

R — Realize what your child needs to know and when.

It can be difficult to assess what sexual information to give your children, how much, and when. There are errors on both sides, of course. Some parents, believing that they are liberating their children from shame and sexual guilt, think nothing of exposing their children to all sorts of sexual media and information. Of course this is rubbish. As Ecclesiastes (3:1) says, "For everything there is a season, and a time for every matter under heaven." This is especially true of giving sexual information. Part of having a healthy sexuality, not to mention a holy one, involves the ability to know how to set sexual boundaries. Exposing children to too much sexual information damages their ability to set those boundaries. Rather than reducing shame and guilt, such parenting strategies tend to produce children who have an indiscriminate attitude toward sexuality, in that they are unable to avoid or even recognize dangerous situations until it is too late.

Jennifer, a client of mine, was raised in such a "liberated" home. Her parents wanted her to be, as she described it, "free to celebrate my sexuality." Jennifer's parents adopted a very permissive attitude toward their daughter's sexual development, regularly exposing her to movies with strong sexual content or to provocative magazines, and, when she was an adolescent, giving her condoms and allowing her to sleep with her boyfriend in their home. Jennifer told me that this was because "my parents thought that kids were going to have sex anyway, so we might as well do it where they knew we were safe."

Unfortunately, this permissiveness caused Jennifer to become too involved too fast with a boy who turned out to be extremely jealous, possessive, and abusive. While there were certainly other factors involved, her lack of sexual boundaries caused her to move too quickly in her relationship, and then, once she was sexually involved, she was unable to break things off with him. As she put it, "I thought, since we were having sex, that meant he loved me. Looking back, I see that he was just using me and I was naïve. My folks had taught me that sex was something beautiful and free that you did whenever you felt you loved someone. I felt I loved him so I had sex with him, but it was anything but beautiful and free. I don't blame my parents for my choices, but I feel a little set up by what they taught me about relationships. It's taken a long time to learn how to trust men again."

Alternatively, some parents, seeking to protect their children's innocence, go to great lengths to shield their children from any sexual information at all. This too is foolish. What these parents forget is that there is a difference between innocence and ignorance. Children raised by parents who mistake the two are easy prey for those looking for a lamb to lead to the slaughter. I am aware of too many young men and women who led seemingly chaste lives while they lived with their parents but became seduced by the atmosphere of alcohol and sex that is alive and well on most college campuses. They simply do not have the tools to cope with these circumstances. Out from under their parents' thumbs, these young adults first treat the sensuality and sin that surrounds them with suspicion, but once their initial shock wears off, they are too easily convinced to join the ride. They become like children set loose in a toy store.

Perhaps a metaphor would help here. If I am at a party and I don't want you to fill my glass with some vile concoction that everyone else is drinking, I shouldn't walk around with an empty glass saying, "No, thank you" to everyone who offers to fill it. If I do, then eventually, just to be polite, I am probably going to be pressured into letting you fill my glass. "After all," I think to myself, "I won't drink it, and at least it will get everyone off my back." But then, having a full glass, I might take a sip, and if it didn't kill me I might take another and then have a second glass, and pretty soon, I am under the table with the rest of the crowd.

No. If I really don't want you to fill my glass, then the best thing I can do is *walk around with a glass full of something else.* This way, if you offer to get me something, I can either say, "Got mine, thanks" or, "Yes, fill me up with more of the same" but I am less likely to change my drink, or mix in anything else that would pollute it.

Do you see where I am going here? Some parents think that to raise a chaste, pure child is to raise an empty child. These parents then send their children out into a world full of people who can't wait to "fill their glasses" with all sorts of poison. If we don't send our children out with some knowledge of those things and give them the simple tools to avoid those poisons, then we will inevitably doom our children. Rather than preventing our children from setting sexual boundaries because they don't know sex can be dangerous (like the parents in the previous example), these parents prevent their children from setting sexual boundaries by pretending that sex doesn't exist. But as soon as these children are shown — usually by some unhealthy source — that sex does indeed exist, thank you very much, their children become seduced by it and lost to it. As far as I am concerned, this is the moral equivalent of throwing your children — who do not know how to swim — into the ocean without a life preserver.

As with all things Catholic, the key is to look for the "Golden Mean" the truth that dwells between the two extremes. If the two extremes are to be avoided — and they are — then it becomes obvious that we must give our children the information

they need when they need it, but not give them so much that
they choke on it. So how do you know when to give your kids
more specific information about sex, reproduction, and morality? I would suggest the following three circumstances.

(a) When they ask for it

This is the most obvious time to give specific sexual information, but sometimes I have encountered parents who are reluctant to answer the direct questions of children who are
deemed "too young." While I would agree that there are certain
ages that it would be inappropriate for the parent to pipe up and
say, "Today I want to talk about sex, so get out your notebook,
my boy," at the same time, if the children are old enough to ask
a specific question, then they are old enough to get a direct,
honest, moral answer. In general, however, I would recommend
that you start with the simplest, least involved answer you can
give and then let the child take the lead for telling you how much
more he or she wants to know. If your three-year-old asks,
"Where do babies come from?" It is enough to start with, "God
gives babies to mommies and daddies." Then simply ask the
child, "Does that answer your question?" If he says "yes," then
your job is done for the moment. If he says "no," then wait pa-
tiently while your child asks his next question (or help him form
the question) and repeat the process. Children are good at letting you know when to stop. As a rule, children are fairly prag-
matic folk, and they don't have patience for a lot of "useless"
information. Chances are, if they ask you a question, it's because
they need to know for some specific reason. But chances are also
that they will tell you when they've got the answers they came
for. Give honest, simple answers, ask them if they need to know
anything else, respond accordingly, and finally, invite them to
come to you with any similar questions in the future.

(b) When your child is displaying some kind of inappropriate behavior

If you observe your child touching him-/herself inappropriately, or looking at pornography, or talking in an immodest manner, or doing any other thing that you would think is either inappropriate or possibly sinful, then your child is old enough to be given information about how to respond to that situation.

At first, it may be enough to kindly but firmly say, "Please don't do that" — for example, with a two-year-old who is touching himself with the same amount of pleasure he gets from picking his nose or examining his ear wax. But if you notice a sexual issue persisting (I won't say sexual problem yet, because my hope is to catch these things before they become actual "problems") — for example, a seven-year-old who is engaging in regular self-touching/masturbation, or a young person who is visiting sexually explicit internet sites or viewing pornography (always assume that the time you catch them isn't the first time), or some other such thing — then it is time to give your child solid moral guidance on these matters, whether or not you think you should have to. Remember, you need to fill their glasses with something good to drink (may I suggest "Living Water"?) before someone else fills it with something else.

(c) When they don't ask, and you wonder why they don't

This is the most delicate area, because the parent runs the risk of giving too much unwanted information if he or she isn't careful. But I raise this issue because we parents need to be as sensitive to the questions our children don't ask as to the ones they do. While there may be a part of you that would be perfectly happy if your child never asked you about anything sexual, the fact is, at each stage of his or her development, it is completely normal to ask certain questions (Part II of this book will address this issue more thoroughly). If your child is not asking these questions and his/her friends are, or certain things you read suggest that he/she "ought to be," it could (and I do mean "could," *not* "would" or "does") indicate a problem. Perhaps the child is afraid to raise the issue. Perhaps he/she is inappropriately oblivious to what's happening in his/her body or around him or her. Perhaps he/she is immature, or perhaps he/she is none of the above and you are fretting over nothing.

Regardless, if you have questions about why your child isn't asking certain questions that, as far as you can ascertain, would be developmentally appropriate, then feel free to casually raise the question yourself. "Have you ever wondered how babies get in their mommies' tummy?" "Do you ever feel pressured by your friends to date or pair up with a boy/girl?" "Do you have any questions about the changes in your body lately?"

Of course, once you've raised the question, you should take the child's lead (see below), but at no time should you feel awkward asking your child for some feedback on the kind of information he or she needs to know and when.

E — Elicit your child's thoughts, attitudes, and ideas.

Any time sexual topics come up, either because your child raised them or you did, it is a good idea to first ask what your child wants to know, or already thinks about the issue at hand. For example:

"Dad, what's oral sex?"
(Pick self up off floor. Take a deep breath.) "Why do you ask, son?"

"Mom, can I get pregnant by kissing a boy?"
"Why do you think so, sweetheart?"

Child: "What does 'get laid' mean?"

Parent (calm self down.): "Wow, that's a very rude expression. What do you think it means?"

"What's a tampon?"

"What makes you ask?"

Asking such questions serves three functions. First, it sends a message of respect to your child. You want to hear what your child thinks on such important matters as sexuality. Granted, you will have to do a lot of correcting and filling in the gaps, but this process works best if it is begun by listening. Second, asking such questions right up front helps you determine exactly what your child wants to know. Finally, it stops you from giving too much information at any given time or reacting too strongly to the topic at hand.

I remember one cartoon several years back in which a child came home from second grade and announced, "Sex, sex, sex! All the teacher ever talks about is sex!" The parents were mortified by this pronouncement and began making plans to complain to the principal and organize the community against this offensive teacher. The next frame of the cartoon showed the child, out of earshot from his parents, muttering under his breath, "Sex plus one is seven. Sex plus two is eight. . . ."

While I doubt anything quite like this would ever happen in real life, it is instructive. When your child asks a question, or a sexual topic is raised, ALWAYS, ALWAYS ALWAYS, ask your child for his or her thoughts and/or clarification before you respond. You could save yourself and your child a lot of work and embarrassment if you do.

S — Speak the truth.

Jesus tells us that the truth will set us free. We would do well to keep this in mind when we talk to our children about sex. When we give children the direct, honest answers they need, we set them free from shame or doubt, and from having to ask less qualified (and less moral) sources for sexual information.

There is nothing wrong with limiting what you tell your child to what he or she needs to know at this particular time of his or her development, but make sure that everything you do say is true and complete, even when it is difficult. Because if you don't, you are setting your child up to ask someone else whose answers you may not approve of.

P — Present a positive, Christian attitude toward sex.

This is extremely important, and I think we have dealt with it extensively already. I will only add this. Your children need to know that Christians are confident, joyful, and respectful of their sexuality. If you do not communicate this message, then you do yourself, your child, and God — the author of sexuality — a disservice. St. John Chrysostom occasionally gave some very beautiful homilies on sexuality. In one, he responds to his critics who are embarrased by his frank talks, *"I know that my words embarrass many of you, and the reason for your shame is your own wanton licentiousness* [N.B.: Here St. John is referring to what I earlier described as the "Narnian apple" phenomenon]. . . . *Some of you call my words immodest, because I speak of the nature of marriage, which is honorable . . . [but] By calling my words immodest, you condemn God, who is the author of marriage."*

Tough talk, but completely true. By presenting a positive, honest image of sexuality to our children, even when it is difficult, we give honor to God, who is the author of our sexuality (and who, in Genesis 1, pronounces it "good"). God will reward our efforts by giving us the grace to raise up healthy, godly, children who exhibit a healthy, godly sexuality.

E — Expect to talk about your own struggles when appropriate.

This is a touchy point, so I want to make sure you understand exactly what I mean. First, under no circumstances am I suggesting that that you lay out all of your sexual exploits for your children to peruse. This would be a gross violation of your children's sexual boundaries, as well as potentially a grave flaunting of a sinful past.

What I do mean, however, is that children have a tendency to follow in the paths of their parents, *even the paths they were not witness to.* For example, I have met many parents who complain, "I used to be an alcoholic, but I was sober long before we had kids, and now I see my kids getting into exactly the same situations I did when I was their age. It's like they are little copies of me."

This is also true of lesser problems. Our habits and histories are often (though not always) re-created in the lives of our children — even when we try to shield them from those habits and histories by concealing them. I will not bore you with the psychological theory that attempts to address this phenomenon; it is enough to know that there isn't much you can hide from your kids even if you try.

The only way to break these patterns is to be honest about them, in as vague a way as possible. If and when it is appropriate, say to your children, "I have had certain struggles with my own sexuality in the past. This is what I have learned, and this is why I am better."

Henry walked in on his fourteen –year-old son masturbating. Of course, they were both mortified, and Henry's first reaction was shock and anger. "I took some time to cool down, though, because I knew how important it was to say the right thing."

Later that day, Henry took a walk with his son, and he did a very brave thing. Henry confided in his son. "I told him that I needed to tell him something that I wanted him to keep between us. I told him that I knew how strong those feelings could be because I used to do that a lot when I was his age. In fact, it became a problem for me that I struggled with for many, many years. I explained that it was embarrassing for me to tell him this, and I wasn't proud of my past in this area, but I wanted him to know how hard it would be to stop later if he kept masturbating, and I didn't want him to be ashamed of himself the way I was for a long time because of my struggle. I explained that God gave him those feelings to draw him closer to his wife someday, and if he kept abusing those feelings, it would make having a good marriage that much harder, because it would make his wife think that he was just using her to satisfy himself, and it could make him think of her that way sometimes too, even if he didn't want to. I offered some suggestions for ways that I learned to gain control of myself. And I told him that I wanted him to do everything he could to not masturbate, because I wanted him to have a happy life, and to have a good relationship where he and his wife could enjoy those kinds of feelings together, the way God intended it."

For the most part, Henry's son just listened, though he did ask one or two questions. But Henry had this to say about the experience. "I think my son expected me to punish him. But realistically, what could I do? Say to him, 'Masturbating? No TV for a week!'? Like that would do any good! Even though it was hard, I thought being honest about my own struggle — without going into it too much — would be the best way to help him avoid the mistakes I made. It was honest, and my son and I ended up taking an upsetting experience and turning it into something that made us feel closer together. Since then, I've noticed he's come to me a lot more to talk about things that were important and personal to him. That's something most of the men I work with say never happens with their sons. What I did was a risk for me. But it seems to be paying off."

If you are going to use this approach with your children, I would offer these closing thoughts. Be honest, but be vague enough not to scandalize or embarrass your child. Finally, concentrate not so much on your struggle as on how you overcame (or are overcoming) that problem, and why your life is so much better now that you are more in control of that part of your life. Remind your child that you are telling him or her this, even though it is hard for you, because you want him or her to have an even happier, healthier life than you have had. And finally, remind your child that, just as he or she would not want you talking about his or her private affairs with your friends, you would prefer that he/she respect your privacy by keeping secret what you shared between the two of you. If you do this, your child will see your honest witness as a gift and respect it as such.

C — Control your temper and the temptation to lecture.

Nothing brings out strong emotions or the temptation to lecture like talking to our kids about sex. Yet both should be avoided as much as possible because both tend to undermine the important lessons we are trying to teach our children.

If we get angry every time we talk about sex or attempt to correct inappropriate displays of our child's sexuality, then we will either foster in our child an unchristian, punitive fear of sexuality, or we will prevent our child from talking to us, or both.

The same is true of lectures. Of course, we must teach, but we must not lecture, because when we lecture, our children's eyes glaze over and they go to that "happy place" in their heads where we don't exist, and everything we say is lost. Rather than lecture, ask questions and then give honest, direct answers. This is the only way to ensure that our children will truly receive the wisdom we have to give.

T — Teach your child what the gift of the body is for.

Throughout the history of Christianity, some groups of otherwise faithful people have struggled with the nature of our bodies. In fact, many groups have tended to denounce the corruption or evil-ness of the body and concentrate exclusively on a more "spiritual" form of Christianity. Whenever this has occurred, the Church has not hesitated to condemn such ideas as heresy. Gnosticism, Manichaeism, Jansenism, Puritanism —all are "wannabe" Christian spiritualities that have been soundly denounced by the Catholic Church time and again.

Yes, we must teach our children to develop mastery over their bodies, including their drives and urges, but we must not do this in a punitive way, as if those drives and urges were evil. After all, they were created by God, who then pronounced his creation "good" (cf. Gen 1:4-31). Rather, we must teach our children what God's intention was when He gave us those drives and urges. God gave us the hunger drive so that we could grow and be strong, and so we do not eat too much because doing so inhibits our growth and strength. In the same way, God gave us our sexual drive to, as the Holy Father tells us, remind us that we were created to give ourselves to others, to work for the good of others. Our sexual drive is really God's way of preventing us from creating little islands of self-sufficiency and dwelling on them

Pope John Paul II's "Theology of the Body" is a beautiful reflection on the gift of the body that God gives to His children.

exclusively. The sexual drive, whether expressed in marriage or channeled into work offered for the good of the world through celibate religious life (incidentally, in both cases, I am referring to a quality psychoanalyst Erik Erikson called "generativity"; that is, sublimation or the harnessing of our sexual energy to create and work for the good of our immediate and extended communities) is God's way of reminding us, as Pope John Paul II wrote in *Familiaris Consortio*, "Love is the fundamental and innate call of every human being."

Teach your child about the goodness of his or her body. Teach your child how to care for his or her body, and how to gain competence with it, which of course includes mastering bodily urges and drives. But make sure that as you do this, you continually remind yourself and your child that his/her body, drives, and urges were given to him/her by God, and we give glory to God (and health to ourselves) when we express those drives and urges in godly, joyful, responsible ways.

The Most Important Thing You Say . . .
Is What You Don't Say

Having reviewed the seven principles that underlie productive discussions about sex with your children, I want to add one more thing. The reason I add it as a postscript is that it is not something you say so much as it is something you do.

If you want to foster a healthy, holy sexuality in your children — if you want to have honest, godly, productive discussions about sexual issues — then you have to build all of these things on a foundation of solid rapport and affection with your children.

The fact is, most of the sexual problems that men and women, both young and old, experience have their roots in a lack of parental affection. To give you two prominent examples, let's look at the biggest struggles men and women have with sexuality. First, we'll take a look at men.

Conventional wisdom teaches that all men want is sex. Men as a general rule have greater problems with masturbation than women, and wives regularly complain that even the most innocent physical affection with their husbands leads to pressure for sex. Popularly it is thought that this is "the way men are."

The fact is that even though many men are this way, it is not how God created men to be. The problems described above do not reflect manhood so much as they reflect a disordered masculinity. So why do so many men exhibit these problems? When babies are born, God gives them a strong need for touch. Babies who are not touched, cuddled, held, and stroked will "fail to thrive." That is, they will refuse even food if their need for touch is not sufficiently being met. This is true of both girl and boy babies, and so we see that in the beginning of life God gives both women and men a strong capacity for affection.

But as male children mature, our fallen society teaches us to stop giving physical affection to our boys for fear of making them into "sissies" or worse. Even so, the male child's need for physical affection — a need given to him by God — does not go away. It is merely repressed, as the affection either stops being offered by the parents, or the child is teased or rebuffed when he reaches out for it. And so the boy learns to bury the need for cuddling which God has hard-wired into his body.

And then comes adolescence. All of a sudden, the male teenager, who has been repressing this need for touch and love, is given permission to touch and be touched — as long as it is in a sexual sphere. The male child then tries to make up for lost time, trying to get all of the touch needs he has missed out on for thirteen, fourteen, fifteen, years, met by using the one tool he has been given permission to use —sex. Of course, even if he finds a sexual partner, no one woman could ever hope to keep up with his insatiable need for touching, a need that goes back to toddlerhood. And so he attempts to make up for this lack of touching from his sexual partner or wife through masturbation, or pornography, or prostitutes, or worse. The result is an emotionally deprived (if not crippled) male who is totally unskilled at relationships but who is also incredibly sexually needy. In my professional experience, I have found that the degree to which a boy was not given affection and affirmation throughout his growing up is directly related to how much he struggles with more and more serious forms of sexual temptation — all in the attempt to meet his God-given need for physical affection, a need thwarted by well-meaning but tragically misguided parents who did not want their sons to grow up to be "affected."

Now let's look at girls. The most common and most feared problem girls face is promiscuity. (Sexual frigidity is the other common problem of female sexuality, but parents at least tend not to fear this to the same degree as raising a child who grows up to be a "tramp.")

If you ask girls who are sexually active why they began sleeping around, almost unanimously they will say, "I wanted someone to love me" or, "I thought that's what I had to do to get him to love me."

Here, too, you see that at the root of the problem is a deep longing for affection. If you gather the history of these girls, you will find that even though many of them come from otherwise fine homes, the one thing that these homes lacked was truly affectionate and emotionally demonstrative mothers and fathers. The girl, looking to meet her God-given need for physical affection and affirmation, is virtually driven to promiscuity by parents — especially fathers — who are stingy with expressions of love.

Even more remarkable it is that if you talk to girls who managed to maintain their virginity — not because they were afraid of their sexuality (as is the case with girls raised in sexually punitive homes) but because they genuinely understood the importance of saving themselves for marriage — you will find that these young women come from homes where open affection is the norm and parent-child rapport is carefully nurtured.

For both boys and girls, a disordered sexuality has its roots in emotionally stingy homes. Boys and girls of every age have deep needs for touch and affirmation, needs given to them by God. If these needs are frustrated for any reason, sexual perversion of one kind of another will result by adolescence and take hold as the years go by. If, on the other hand, these needs are met consistently, generously, and to the degree that the individual child needs them to be met (as opposed to merely the degree to which the parent is comfortable meeting them), then that child will be on the road to having a healthy, holy sexuality.

Mind you, I'm not suggesting that by giving your child all the affection and affirmation he or she needs, you are guaranteeing that he or she will be both sexually healthy and chaste, but I am saying that you increase their chances exponentially. Think of it this way: Imagine taking a dish towel and submerging it in a glass of water. Pretty soon, that dish towel will have absorbed all of the water into itself. But what would happen if you first sprayed that dishcloth with a water-resistant fabric coating like ScotchGuard and then submerged the cloth in the glass of water? Chances are it would absorb some of the water, but not nearly the same amount as if you left it completely unprotected.

In a sense, affection and affirmation are the ScotchGuard of our children's sexuality. Like it or not, at some point our children are going to be submerged in the hypersexual world around them. It simply cannot be avoided (though exposure should be limited to whatever reasonable degree it is possible for a parent to do so). Yet, how much of that culture our children absorb is directly dependent upon how well our children have been made "water-resistant" by a liberal and ample application of physical affection and affirmation on our part. Yes, they may absorb — in spots — some of the culture that surrounds them, but they will not become soggy with that culture like their peers who were deprived of the affection and affirmation they were created by God to need.

If you don't remember anything else from this chapter, remember this. Give your girls and boys the affection and affirmation they crave, so that you can create a strong foundation for all the other good things this book, and your own wisdom, have to offer your child.

Part Two:

Ages and Stages of Sexuality

Over the next few chapters, you will discover how to foster a healthy and holy sexuality in your children over the years as we explore infancy and toddlerhood, childhood (which, together with infancy and toddlerhood, encompass what Pope John Paul II has referred to as "the years of innocence"), puberty, and adolescence leading into young adulthood.

As you will see, each stage has its challenges and its rewards as well as its critical lessons. Even if your children are older, I would encourage you to read the chapters that precede the ones that are most relevant to you, so that you can see how each lesson builds on the others. But if you are coming into these lessons midway through your parenting career, don't despair or think that it's too late for you. It is never too late to begin fostering a godly sexuality in yourself and/or your children. Read all of the chapters to fill in the gaps in your own knowledge, but apply the parts that are most applicable to your own life.

Let's begin our journey through childhood.

CHAPTER FOUR

Laying the Foundation

Infancy, Toddlerhood, and Early Childhood
(Birth to Age Four)

It might seem strange to some readers to speak of the sexuality of an infant, toddler, or youngest child, and it would be strange to speak of it in the genital sense, since infants and toddlers are not really in a genital or erotic stage of development.

But infants and toddlers do have critical lessons to learn, such as developing an appreciation for and mastery over their bodies, becoming grounded in love and touch, and many other matters, including the following:

- Learning basic trust, which in later life will allow them to delay gratification when necessary.
- Learning the donative meaning of the body through parental modeling.
- Mastering basic bodily functions and learning the goodness of their bodies, which sets the stage for future self-mastery and healthy body-sense.
- Learning that God is the author of all life, which is a beautiful gift.
- Answering questions about basic physical differences between boys and girls.

- Learning safe and appropriate ways to express emotions.
- Learning to respect the healthy, appropriate boundaries set by parents.

Let's take a closer look at each of these.

Learning Basic Trust

Basic trust is the first lesson any child must learn if he or she is to be able to develop healthy personhood. Trust is essential for hope to flourish (because it allows me to trust that tomorrow may be better than today); it is the foundation of faith (because it tells me that I can count on others, including God, the Supreme Other); it is the seat of one's ability to delay gratification (because I trust that even if I don't get it right now, it can still be gotten at some future point); and it serves as the predictor of how a child will respond to authority (because respect for authority is dependent upon my ability to trust you to look out for my best interests).

A healthy sense of trust sets the stage for a healthy sexuality because in order to live a chaste life:

- I must be able to hope that someday God will either provide me a mate or give me the grace to live a celibate life.
- I must have a strong faith, so that my faith informs not just my religious practice, but the way I live my life, and I can't have a strong faith unless I can trust that God is looking out for my best interests, and His word is my joy.
- I must be able to delay gratification, trusting that there is a benefit in waiting to fulfill the sexual urges I will one day experience.
- I must be able to trust and respect the authority of those who give me information on how to foster a healthy and holy sexuality as I grow.

So how do you foster basic trust from infancy? By responding to a child's cries quickly and consistently. Studies have shown that children whose cries are not attended to in this manner are at much higher risk for depression, both in the immediate and distant future.

There is a great deal of lousy parenting advice that suggests the benefits of letting the infant "cry it out" to promote independence, but this is faulty logic. Independence cannot be forced on a child. By definition, independence must be taken by the child, and the child will not be ready to take that independence unless he or she is confident that he/she has a secure base to work from.

Responding to a child's cries quickly and consistently lets that child know that when he calls, he will be answered, which fosters a secure base for him to launch from. While it is true that the child does not learn everything he needs to know about trust at this stage — that, in fact, trust unfolds over the years — a precedent is set at this stage which the parents and children will probably follow for the rest of their lives. Parents who respond quickly and consistently to their child's cries at this stage set a precedent for responding sensitively to their child's concerns, as opposed to parents who do not respond as quickly, who are more likely to send the message that they would prefer that their children figure things out for themselves. While "figuring things out for themselves" sounds good on the surface, it can also be detrimental, as when a child is left to figure out his own sexuality without appropriate guidance. By contrast, the parent who responds quickly and consistently to his child's needs from birth learns to read what his child needs at any

For more information, see my book *Parenting with Grace: The Catholic Parent's Guide to Raising (almost) Perfect Kids.*

given moment. Sometimes the child will need to figure things out for him-/herself; sometimes the child will need to work with the parent to figure things out, but knowing the difference requires a parent to respond attentively in the first place.

By using those parenting methods that promote attentive, responsive parenting, we foster the trust necessary for a healthy and holy sexuality.

Learning the donative meaning of the body through parental modeling

Through his "Theology of the Body," Pope John Paul II teaches us that the reason God gave us bodies is primarily to be able to work for the good of others. This is what the Church calls the "donative meaning of the body."

Catholic parents are called to model the donative meaning of the body to their children as a way of teaching their children by example. If we want our children to learn that our bodies are not intended to be used for selfish ends, then we must show our children, from the earliest age, how to use one's body generously to work for the good of another.

When parents practice such parenting activities as extended nursing, co-sleeping (a.k.a. "the family bed"), and "baby wearing" (that is, keeping the youngest child close at all times by carrying him or "wearing" him close to the body in a "baby sling") we teach by example the donative meaning of the body. Parents may want to use their bodies in less donative ways. We may want to encourage our children to use things to comfort themselves instead of us; however, when we do this, we not only violate the donative meaning of our own bodies, but we also serve as a poor example to our children that their bodies should be used, not primarily as instruments of their own gratification, but as instruments through which they work for the good of another. Furthermore, we encourage our children to develop a materialistic attitude (i.e.,"things are a good substitute for intimacy") when we deny our children the comfort of our bodies and instead push blankies, binkies, and other "transitional objects" onto them. While I am not suggesting that the child who uses a pacifier will grow up to be some kind of sexual deviant (that would be ridiculous to say), I am saying that the example you set today determines the credibility you will have tomorrow. You can't pull "the donative meaning of the body" out of the air when your children are adolescents and expect them to appreciate the concept if you have not used your own body for their good from the earliest stages of their lives.

But if you have used the parenting methods I mentioned above, when you want to teach your child about the donative meaning of the body, all you have to do is say, "Remember how I nursed you for so long and you stayed in our bed, and I carried you so much? Well, there were lots of times that I got tired, or wanted to put you in a crib, or give you a binky and set you in a play pen, but I didn't because I knew that God wanted me to use my body to do the things you needed me to do for you. And you know what? I think we grew a lot closer because of that.

"Now that you are getting older, you need to learn more about how to use your own body to work for the good of others too. . . ."

You can then go on to give examples of how to do this. For the young child, that will mean doing what he or she can to help around the house and offering comfort to his/her brothers and sisters as he/she is best able. For an older child, that will mean doing all of the things I mentioned already, plus treating friends with respect and offering service to the community.

For the adolescent, it will mean all of that plus treating boy-/
girl friends with honor and respect, always seeking to treat them
as a person, a child of God, and not some object.

Again, a proper understanding of the donative meaning of
the body unfolds over the years, but the stage is set now. Use
parenting methods that model the meaning of the body, and
you will have the credibility you need to insist that your children be willing to use their bodies to work for the good of
another, whether in a sexual sphere or otherwise.

Mastering basic bodily functions and learning the goodness of their bodies, which sets the stage for future self-mastery and healthy body-sense

Bodily mastery is an important challenge of the early years
of life. Learning that one's body and bodily functions are good,
and how to gain mastery over the same, sets the stage for a
healthy sense of personhood.

The child seeks to gain mastery first over her limbs, then
her bowels, and then language. The wise parent will be encouraging and patient, and set gentle limits as the child makes
many innocent mistakes on the road to bodily competence.

Use this time to teach your child the goodness of his body. As
he is learning to walk, say out loud, "Thank you, God, for giving
(baby's name) such strong legs." When he is toilet training, after
you compliment your child for a job well done you should not
feel at all strange saying, "Thank you, God, for giving (baby's
name) a healthy body and teaching him how to use it."

Being sensitive to your child's development and neither
rushing nor hindering your child's attempts to gain bodily mastery are extremely important to laying the foundation for a
healthy sexuality. The person whose sexuality is healthy is com-

fortable with the body God gave him, which requires knowing what he is capable of, knowing his limits, and being patient with both.

Learning that God is the author of all life, which is a beautiful gift

Having a healthy respect for life — all life — is an important part of a healthy and holy sexuality. Begin fostering that respect for life now. Young children have a fascination with babies. They will frequently point to an infant and squeal with glee and wonderment, "BAY-BEE!" Encourage this. Say out loud, "Isn't God wonderful for making babies? Thank you, God, for babies!"

Every day, let your child know that he or she is God's gift to you. Regardless of the day you have had with your child, during prayers, thank the Lord "for the gift of my son/daughter (name)." Tell your child of his/her worth to you, as well as his/her spiritual worth every day, and model that worth in the importance you place upon maintaining an intimate family life. Such actions are the foundation of a respect for life. Knowing that you were wanted — and how much — makes it unfathomable to think that any child could possibly be unwanted. I do not think that I am being naïve to suggest that if pro-choice adults felt more wanted by their own parents (both because of their parent's word and example) they would not be as readily "pro-choice." But don't take my word for it. Ask some pro-choice persons to describe their growing up years, and you will find ample evidence that he or she was given either an implicit or explicit message that he or she was a burden, and therefore, parents should be given the "right" to ease their burden — by whatever means they see fit.

Children are hard work, and there is nothing wrong with acknowledging that. But don't ever treat your child in a way that makes him or her think that he or she is a burden (though not necessarily unwanted), and that includes things like workaholism (which gives the impression that children inhibit careers), overly harsh discipline, stingy affection, and name-calling — in addition to the more obvious things like saying "You were an accident" or "We never wanted you" — because if you do, you will undermine the ethic of life upon which a healthy sexuality stands.

Answering questions about genitality and the basic physical differences between boys and girls

The first questions about anatomical differences between boys and girls often come in late toddlerhood and early child-hood. It is very important to prepare yourself to answer such questions simply, honestly, and pleasantly.

My recommendation is not to wait until your child asks the questions, but try to prepare some answers for the most com-mon questions ahead of time. "Why do boys and girls look different?" "How come daddy is so hairy?" "Why doesn't mommy have a penis?" "Where do babies come from?" To these questions, the simple answers are the best:

"Why do boys and girls look different?"
"Because God made them different."

"How come daddy is so hairy?"
"Because when boys get older they get hairier."

"Why doesn't mommy have a penis?"
"Because God made her body different from daddy's."

"Where do babies come from?"

"Babies come from God, and he gives them to mommies and daddies to love."

If your child wants to know more, help your child find the words he/she needs to ask the questions, and give similar, direct, simple answers to those questions as well.

When teaching your child about body parts, I would encourage you to use actual names. Just like you call hair "hair," and a mouth "a mouth" and you don't make up juvenile, giggle-inducing names for those parts; there is nothing wrong with the use of words like "penis," "vagina," or "urethra." Frankly, these words beat the dickens out of "wiener," "pee-hole," or any of the other gosh-awful names that otherwise well-meaning parents give to their children's private parts.

Using nicknames for genitals is an understandable attempt to diffuse parental awkwardness about sexuality, but I would suggest that using such names does our sexuality a disservice by reinforcing the idea that we should be embarrassed by the noble, proper name of a thing. Plus, as our children grow and learn the appropriate names for those parts of the body, they will tend to look patronizingly at their parents, who seem to appear so backward about their own sexuality that they can't even bring themselves to say the words. For example, what adolescent in his right mind wants to get sexual advice from a parent who taught him to call his penis a "wee-wee?"

Regardless, late toddlerhood/early childhood is also the time to teach lessons about basic modesty. This is the time to teach our children that the parts covered by a bathing suit are private and should not be exposed, or touched in public. This is not because these parts are not good, but just as the best presents are kept in wrapping paper, the most special parts of ourselves are kept "wrapped up" in clothes, and we only show those parts to the special and important people —like a mommy or daddy (or sometimes a doctor), and in adulthood, a husband or a wife — whom God has given to us to take care of us and love us. Likewise, it is a good idea to teach your children that the words used to describe their private parts are special and important words that should only be spoken about to a some-one who is as special or important, like a mommy, a daddy, a doctor, or a husband or wife. The latter rule is an attempt to prevent one's child from climbing on top of a picnic table at the family reunion and announcing that "My vagina is itchy!"

While we are on the topic of itchy privates, this might be a good time to address the issue of genital touching, which often occurs in late toddlerhood and early childhood. At this stage, I prefer not to use the word masturbation because of the connotations, but call it what you like. Toddlers are engaged in the work of seeking independence, but sometimes independence is scary, so they need to hold something that makes them feel good. Let's face it. Genital touching feels good.

Even so, it is inappropriate. But it is up to the parent to *gently* redirect the child engaged in this behavior and *not* come across like the child is engaging in some kind of ritual satanic sacrifice.

If you see your toddler touching himself or herself, it is enough to say "No, thank you, honey, we don't touch ourselves that way," and then offer another way for the child to feel comforted. For example; scooping him up in your arms, tickling him and telling him that you love him, or encouraging him to play a particular game he enjoys, or asking him to find his favorite stuffed animal to cuddle. Incidentally, these same recommendations work for girls as well as boys.

As I said above there is no need to become apoplectic about toddler genital touching, but it is a concern for Catholics, and as the Vatican said in *The Truth and Meaning of Human Sexuality*, "From the earliest age, parents may observe the beginning of genital sexual activity in their child. It should not be considered repressive to *correct such habits gently* that could become sinful later, and, when necessary, to teach modesty as the child grows [italics ours]."

A child's sexuality is present from the earliest stages of life, and this is a good and beautiful thing. However, it is up to Catholic parents to train their child's sexuality the same way they train their child's will. Gently, lovingly, and consistently.

Learning safe and appropriate ways to express emotions

Because having a healthy sexuality is not just about learning how to express one's body to another person, but also one's spirit and mind, it is important to begin teaching the art of emotional expression (and control) at the earliest opportunity.

While an infant may experience strong emotions, the child's capacity for emotional expression and emotional control really doesn't emerge until the child begins gaining some skill with language. Around the time your child begins developing some ability to communicate, you will need to do several things to help her learn to express and control her emotions properly.

For example: When your child tries to hit, bite, or kick, teach him to "use your words." Teach him what to say in order to express his anger or frustration appropriately; ask him to repeat the words you have given him, and reward him with affection and approval when he does this to your satisfaction. When your child hugs you, tell him you love him and encourage him to say those words to you. Teach your child to identify his feelings by labeling them when you see them ("Wow, that face tells me that you are angry/happy/sad/frustrated/etc."). This activity, done in many contexts throughout the course of a child's lifetime, gives rise to a child who knows how to use words, instead of just his body, to express emotions like anger, and love. Too many children, especially male children, are not trained in the art of giving words to their feelings. Because of this, *they have no choice* but to express themselves physically: "When I feel angry, I fight. When I feel loving, I have sex." These inappropriate displays of perfectly appropriate feelings are the direct result of having been raised by parents who did not teach their children to "use their words" and instead tolerated immature physical expressions of emotion.

Teach your children how to achieve intimacy and solve problems with words, and you will decrease the chances that they will be forced to use their bodies at inappropriate times and in unacceptable ways to express those same emotions. For more tips on teaching your children to express their emotions respectfully, see *Parenting with Grace*.

Learning to respect the healthy, appropriate boundaries set by parents

It is my contention — based on years of clinical observation —that parental love and authoritativeness (though not authoritarianism) must be well established by early childhood. If your child is not confirmed in your love for him or is not taught to respect your authority by early childhood, then you will be fighting an uphill battle with your child for the rest of his life no matter what you do. That is not to say that your child will never listen to you, just that your child will be more likely to give you grief when you ask him to do the least thing — or attempt to advise him on any topic — if you have not showered that child with love and also demonstrated that you have the ability to cause him to comply with your directions — whether he likes it or not — by early childhood.

In *Parenting with Grace*, my wife and I spend many chapters on how to set and enforce appropriate limits, but to be frank, there is too much involved in that process to get into it here. Suffice it to say that you must begin setting reasonable, logical, firm, loving boundaries at this age and use your greater intelligence to cause the child to comply. If you do not find ways to do this, your child will lack the respect for you that is required if he is to take your advice on sexual development seriously.

Onward Ho!

In the next section, we will look at middle and late childhood with an eye toward the lessons that will need to be taught in order to nurture your children's healthy and holy sexual development.

CHAPTER FIVE

The Years of Innocence

Middle and Late Childhood

A child is in the stage described . . . as "the years of innocence" from about five years of age until puberty. . . .
Nonetheless, this period of childhood is not without its
own significance in terms of psycho-sexual development.
A growing boy or girl is learning what it means to be a
woman or a man. Certainly, expressions of natural ten-
derness should not be discouraged among boys, nor
should girls be excluded from vigorous physical activity. . . . [Also,] parents should encourage a spirit of generosity and self-denial in their children, as well as a capacity
for self-reflection and sublimation. . . . Parents should
present objective standards of what is right and wrong,
thereby creating a sure moral framework for life.

~The Pontifical Council on the Family,
The Truth and Meaning of Human Sexuality

As *The Truth and Meaning of Human Sexuality* tells us, the years
of middle and late childhood are important for sexual formation
because they are the primary time for developing gender identity
and learning gender roles. It is also the most active time for conscience formation and emotional/intellectual development.

Regarding this last point, the child must use the years between early childhood and puberty to learn how to place his intellect in the driver's seat over his emotions and urges. That is not to say that he should repress those drives and urges (they are, after all, given to him by God). Rather, he must learn to use his intellect to find godly, respectful, and efficient ways to express those natural emotions. In fact, in the quote above, the word "sublimation" is used. That is a psychological term which refers to the process a person uses to find appropriate ways to express inappropriate urges. For example, if someone cuts me off in traffic, almost killing me and my family, my initial reaction might be to entertain some James Bond fantasy of chasing him down, running him off a cliff, and cackling wildly while his car bursts into flames (and I know I'm not the only one who occasionally thinks like this; I've seen *you* drive). This, however, would be inappropriate — to say the least. So instead I *sublimate* that urge into muttering under my breath, or on a good day I may even pray for that person. Both of these are examples of sublimation. I use my intellect to find moral and socially acceptable ways to express an otherwise sinful, destructive, or inappropriate urge.

In addition to the above, there are several lessons about chastity and sexuality to be learned at this stage of a child's development. These include:

- Continuing to facilitate emotional mastery
- Modeling good relational skills
- Taking steps to foster healthy conscience formation
- Facilitating gender identification by building relationship with the same-sex parent
- Handling early questions about sex
- Setting appropriate but gentle limits around masturbatory activity

Over the next few pages, we will take a closer look at each of the above.

Continue to facilitate emotional mastery

In the last chapter, we talked about the importance of helping your children use their intellect and language to express their emotions through techniques such as labeling your child's feelings, asking your child to repeat things that he or she says more respectfully, helping the child find words to express emotions (instead of fists, feet, and acts of physical aggression), and using time-outs when necessary to help a child calm down enough to express her-/himself respectfully.

In this stage of your child's development, it will be important for you to continue giving your child the words he needs to express himself respectfully, and encouraging him to "use those words" instead of his body to express emotion. For example, many children, around the age of seven or eight, go through a phase where tantrums suddenly begin rearing their ugly heads again. The parent encountering such displays must do two things. First, she must let it be known in no uncertain terms that such eruptions will not be tolerated. In the presence of such fits, the parent should give the child one opportunity to get him- or herself under control, and if the child is unsuccessful, then it is completely appropriate to require the child to go to his or her time-out place (preferably not the child's room, as there are too many distractions there) until he or she has regained control. Then, the parent must do the second thing. Teach the child how he or she should handle that situation next time, even to the point of rehearsing it when necessary. *Parenting with Grace* goes into much more detail for handling tantrums at different stages of your child's development. The point here is not to give you a primer on tantrums. Rather, I want to give you an illustration of the importance of teaching your child how to use intellect and language to guide emotions. If you don't, you will end up with an impulsive child who is unable to control any of his drives, least of all his sexuality. On the other hand, if you are too heavy-handed with regard to your child's emotional displays — for example, spanking her for crying "too much" ("That's right, keep crying, and I'll give you something to cry about!") or calling the child names because of her outburst ("You are such a brat!") — you will end up with a repressed child who will either use his or her sexuality to rebel against you, or be hopelessly crippled when it is his or her turn to express emotions and sexuality with a marriage partner.

The trick to teaching healthy emotional expression and control is to (1) stop the outburst quickly, using the least offensive tools available to you (for example, a warning or time out), and (2) after the child is calmer, teach her what she should have done even to the point of rehearsing how the child must respond to a similar situation in the future. Following these two steps (combined with ample parental affection and affirmation) will help you raise children who know how to channel their emotional energy without turning into emotionally crippled adults.

Model good relational skills

Because the entire point of discipline and parenting is to teach your children how to have healthy relationships with others, your marriage is the most important parenting tool you have for teaching your children, especially when it comes to teaching them how to relate to the opposite sex.

The truth is, the healthier your marriage, the easier it will be to discipline your children and raise them to be healthy men and women, because you will not look like a hypocrite to your child. This is not to say that it is impossible to practice good discipline in the absence of a solid marriage relationship, just that it can make things more difficult and may undermine some of the more subtle lessons you are trying to teach. Considering all of the above, it would be wise to take time for the regular care and feeding of your relationship.

To this end, one of the most beneficial exercises I give to couples in counseling is something I call a "Love List." That is, when a husband and wife write down as many simple things as they can think of that make them feel loved or attended to when their partner does them. The simpler, the better. For example: "I love when we sit on the same piece of furniture together instead of across the room from each other." "I love when you give me a meaningful kiss before you leave instead of just a peck on the cheek." "It means a lot when you put down the newspaper and look at me when I talk to you." "I love when you hold my hand in public or call me from work just to say 'I love you.'" And so on.

Once you have completed your lists, exchange papers. Make yourselves responsible for doing as many of the items on your mate's list as possible every day. Not only does this benefit the marriage in many ways that will surprise you; it will help to ensure that you are presenting many valuable lessons to your children about marriage, without even having to say them directly. Lessons such as:

- Good relationships require constant attention and loving effort.
- The more effort you expend on keeping a relationship strong, the more loving you feel.

- Love is not primarily a feeling; it is a work, a choice, an action.
- It is important to do the things that are meaningful to your mate, whether or not they are meaningful to you.
- There is no place for selfishness in marriage.
- Even when you are busy, it is important to make time to love your partner.
- Plus, you will raise your children in a home that feels secure and warm. Giving your children such a loving model to follow in their own marriages is key to fostering their sexuality, because it shows that sexuality must flow from friendship.

Take steps to foster healthy conscience formation

Middle childhood is the time for seeing to the healthy development of your child's conscience. Obviously, a healthy conscience is key to a healthy sexuality, because without such a conscience, your child will be unable to make moral decisions. The following represent some of the lessons you will need to pass on to teach your child to have a healthy conscience.

1. It is important to do what *is* right, not just what *feels* right.

Feelings are tricky. On the one hand, they must be respected as gifts from God because when they are working properly, they are like our early warning lights that tell us when something might be wrong. On the other hand, feelings are the most unreliable sources of information and the easiest to break down. Let me offer an illustration.

On the dashboard of every car are things called "idiot lights" that tell you when you are low on oil, or when a headlight is out, or alert you to any number of potential problems with your vehicle. Now, I am a person who is a complete idiot when it comes to cars. People, I know. Cars? They're another story. Anyway, those idiot lights can be very helpful for a person like me, who thinks that the best way to fix the car is to turn up the radio so you don't have to hear the scraping noise coming from the engine anymore.

But I also know that those idiot lights tend to be the most sensitive parts on a car. It is not uncommon that they would become stuck on, or short out. If I were completely reliant on them to tell me when to take care of my car, I might be constantly adding oil when I didn't really need it (if the light was stuck on) or never adding oil at all (because the light shorted out). I have to educate myself about my car enough to know that I should check my engine or my oil or my fuel level even when the lights are telling me something else by their presence or absence.

In the same way, emotions are the "idiot lights" on the human dashboard. We should be grateful for them, they often give useful information, but they are the most susceptible to breakdown. And if I only rely on them to tell me what to do, then often I will make unhealthy choices.

Teach your children to have a healthy respect for their feelings, but teach them that their feelings will not always guide them properly.

2. A healthy conscience requires an objective standard.

So, if you can't go on your feelings alone, what do you rely on? You need an objective standard. For example, if the oil light on my car doesn't work, I am going to ask my mechanic how often I should check and change my oil. And if I want to keep my car in good working order, then I will do what my mechanic says, whether or not I understand it, and whether or not the "idiot lights" on my dashboard agree with his schedule. I respect and follow his counsel because he is an acknowledged expert in the field.

In the same way, if we want to keep our minds and souls in healthy working order, then we need to find an expert who can counsel us on matters of morality. An expert to whom we will then give more credence than the "idiot lights" of our emotions. We may not understand everything the Divine Mechanic (i.e., the Church) says, but if we are wise, we will do what she says, not because we are mindless drones who must do what the Church tells us or else, but because she has two thousand years of experience fixing souls and has been accredited as an "expert" in such matters by the Son of God Himself.

Of course, I am free to learn more about why the Church teaches what she does. I am free to struggle to understand why she teaches what she does insofar as she is a patient mechanic and is able to tolerate and answer all the questions I care to ask. I am even free to reject her advice, if I prefer to follow the idiot lights of my emotions for example, but if we put all the pride and politics aside, I think most intelligent people would admit that when we reject the advice of an expert with two thousand years of expertise in her field, we do so at our own peril.

There is an old saying in the legal profession: "The man who serves as his own lawyer has a fool for a client." If this is true, then it would be even more true to say, "The man who serves as his own master has a fool for a disciple." Teach your child what the Church has to say about faith and morals. Teach it as the truth, because it is the truth. And teach these moral and spiritual principles as things to which we need to submit, whether we feel like it or not — because, as C.S. Lewis has observed, Christianity is not about validating my opinions or proving my feelings correct; it is about "unconditional surrender. Throwing down my arms and following Christ." That, of course, includes following the teachings of the Church Christ established and invested His own authority in.

3. Teach your children to pray for wisdom and prudence.

But even for the faithful Catholic who is committed to following the teachings of the Church, there are a million moral questions that you can't simply look up in the catechism. You have to use your intellect and spirit to prayerfully consider the teachings of the Church and apply them to the unique circumstances you find yourself in. The Church is not, as some silly people have accused her of being, some taskmaster who seeks to supplant our own brains with slavish doctrine. Rather, the Church is a guide who maps out the safe paths we can follow to get up the mountain. But we are still responsible for choosing which of those paths we are best suited for, making sure we watch our steps along the way and get ourselves up that mountain.

Because of this, we must teach our children to pray for wisdom and prudence in all things. Wisdom is the virtue that allows us to discern God's will for our unique circumstances. Prudence, then, is the virtue that allows us to find the best methods to apply that wisdom to our unique circumstances. Wisdom allows us to discern the truth. Prudence allows us to find ways to live in the truth while still being respectful to others on the path.

The balance between the two can be a tricky one, but it is a balance that God will help us and our children to strike if we pray.

4. Rehearse moral dilemmas.

As your children get older, give them stories of age-appropriate moral dilemmas to wrestle with. For example: A boy is angry with another boy in class. What should he do? A girl sees something she wants in the store, but she doesn't have the money to buy it. How could she handle that — especially if she really, really wants it right now and her mom said, "no"? There are a million examples of moral dilemmas you can "play" with. But don't just give your child a problem to struggle with and then leave him to his own devices. Give him a story problem and also give him some parameters to work in. For example: What would be the most generous thing to do? What would be the most honest answer? How could you do what's right and still be sensitive to the others around you who disagree? How could you do what's right even if the others continued to disagree?

Rehearsing such situations does not guarantee that your child will automatically do those things if the temptation would ever arise, but it gets his or her mind heading in the right direction. Likewise, grounding your child in Scripture and the lives of the saints provides excellent examples of what it takes to exhibit moral courage.

While there is much more that could be said about this subject, it is my hope that the above can serve as an outline for you to follow when fostering the development of your child's conscience.

Facilitate gender identification by building relationship with the same-sex parent

This is a big one. In fact, this is the main job of middle childhood: learning what it means to be a man or woman. And just to make sure we get it right, I want to revisit a quote from *The Truth and Meaning of Human Sexuality*.

> A growing boy or girl is learning from adult example and family experience what it means to be a woman or man. Certainly, expressions of natural tenderness and sensitivity should not be discouraged among boys, nor should girls be excluded from vigorous physical activities. On the other hand, in some societies subjected to ideological pressures, parents should also protect themselves from an exaggerated opposition to what is defined as the *stereotyping of roles*. The real differences between the two sexes should not be ignored or minimized, and in a healthy family environment children will learn that it is natural for certain differences to exist between the usual family and domestic roles of men and women. [italics in original]

As the quote above suggests (especially when taken in the greater context of Pope John Paul II's "Theology of the Body" and the Vatican's teaching on the complementarity of men's and women's roles) it is important that we always remember that there is both a common humanity that unites men and women *and* there are important differences between men and women, but the real *differences that exist between men and women enable them to work more effectively as "helpmates" while the false differences cause them to feel*

Without getting into a heavy-duty theological discussion (alternatively, if you would like more reading on this subject, I would encourage you to read *For Better...FOREVER!*, *Marriage: The Rock on Which the Family is Built*, and *The Original Unity of Man and Woman. A Catechesis on the Book of Genesis* in ascending order of difficulty), I want to help you understand how to discern the real versus the false differences between men and women so that you can pass on to your children the Truth of the Church as you seek to raise up Christian men and women.

estranged from one another. As we teach our children what it means to be men and women, we must be careful not do anything that on the one hand exaggerates the differences between men and women and offends the humanity that unites us. On the other hand, we must be careful to not do anything to take away from the real differences that exist between men and women.

False differences between men and women are the result of the Fall of Adam and Eve. These differences represent those things that stand in the way of the Original Unity that Adam and Eve experienced in each other's presence (As it is written in Genesis [2:23], "This at last is bone of my bones and flesh of my flesh.") So, for example, any time a man says, "Men aren't emotional" or, "Men are oversexed" or, "Men aren't supposed to take care of children or keep the home" — or a woman says, "Women aren't sexual" or, "Women aren't good with logic" or, "Women aren't supposed to do anything with the finances, or yardwork" — they are actually offending both the generosity that a good Christian marriage requires and the common humanity that unites men and women. They are denying certain gifts that God has given them by virtue of their humanity, which serves as the foundation for true masculinity or femininity.

On the other hand, any time both a man and a woman meet all of the tasks, jobs, and challenges of everyday life together, bringing to bear on the task *the unique perspectives and skills that their genders afford them*, then these differences — the real differences between men and women — allow them to experience a greater unity and partnership. For example, a man and a woman might approach the rearing of children, or the managing of money, or the running of the home, or any number of things from somewhat different perspectives, but if both of them apply their full effort to such tasks — in the unique ways their bodies and minds allow them — and respond respectfully to the unique perspectives their mate offers, the tasks are done more efficiently, the relationship between them becomes more intimate, and the diversity and common humanity between men and women are celebrated. In short, the real differences between men and women enable a couple to work better together *because* of those differences — like two experts who bring unique but compatible skills to bear on a problem, while false differences make men and women feel as if they come from two different planets and the best they can hope for is to learn to tolerate the foreign ways of thinking and behaving that each one manifests. To put it another way, the attitude that says, "Men are from Mars and Women are from Venus" stands in direct opposition to the teachings of the Church.

The fact is, the Holy Father teaches that when God created Adam and Eve, He gave all of Himself, His love, His logic, His creativity, His nurturance, His communicativeness — in fact, all the qualities we consider to be human goods — into both men and women. Then He created men's and women's bodies to emphasize different aspects of those same qualities. Only by acknowledging our common humanity and acknowledging the unique ways our bodies allow us to live out that common humanity are we able to be true men and women of God and raise true men and women of God to celebrate the real differences that exist between the genders without lapsing into the false ones.

So, now that the theory is out of the way, how exactly do we raise children to be godly men and women? Consider the following seven tips as your outline.

1. Be a good spouse.

We touched on this above, but it bears repeating. Men and women were created to love each other, to serve each other, to work for each other's good on a daily basis. Celebrating a true masculinity or femininity in your own life and teaching the same to your children are directly dependent upon your ability to first be the spouse your mate needs you to be, the spouse Christ commands you to be, the spouse Christ Himself would be. Assuming that your mate is not asking for something that offends your God-given, kingly dignity or your morality, then you are obliged to respond generously to anything your spouse says he or she needs from you — whether or not you feel like doing it, whether or not it makes you uncomfortable, whether or not you feel that he or she deserves such generosity. Being a true man or woman means being a true helpmate, and helpmates do not refuse to give help or themselves in any way that is required.

Model this generosity for your children, and encourage them to manifest this same generosity with their brothers and sisters and friends.

2. Spend time with your same-sex child.

Masculinity and femininity are not so much taught as caught. You cannot preach lessons on being a man or being a woman to your child. You must live out your own masculinity or feminity and allow your children to work alongside you while you do it. Make time to work and play with your children, especially with the children who share your sex, so that they can learn what it means to be a man or woman of God in an experiential way, not just an intellectual one.

3. Spend time with your children of the opposite sex.

An important part of learning to be a man or a woman involves learning how to expect that one should be treated by the opposite sex. You can do a lot to foster a healthy sense of male-female relationships not only by having a good marriage, but by having regular father-daughter or mother-son "dates."

On such outings, boys and girls will bond with their parents, of course, but more importantly, they will learn how to treat and be treated by a healthy member of the opposite sex. Girls who are regularly treated to one-on-one time with respectful, faithful, strong, and affectionate fathers will be less likely to date abusive, disrespectful, demeaning, or, for that matter, milquetoast men in their adolescence. Boys who are regularly treated to one-on-one time with their strong, respectful, faithful, affectionate mothers will be less likely to date shrewish and disrespectful, or, for that matter, mousy and mindless girls in their adolescence.

Make time for those special father-daughter, mother-son dates and you will be setting a standard for your own children in their future romantic relationships.

4. Encourage same-gender play.

At this age, boys and girls tend to naturally gravitate toward their own gender for play. This is perfectly acceptable and should be encouraged by setting up regular play dates with other children who can serve as peer examples of your family's faith, beliefs, and morality.

5. Discourage negative characterizations of the opposite gender.

One of the negative and false characteristics that results from the desire of children at this stage to play with members of the same sex is often a prejudice toward likes and activities of the opposite sex. It is not uncommon for boys to taunt each other with, "That's a girl thing!" or girls to say, "That's a boy thing!" as if those activities, toys, or interests were somehow bad or disgusting.

This is an example of the estrangement between men and women at its most innocent and basic level. But innocent though it may be, it is still a false difference as it sets the stage for future estrangement. The boy who looks down his nose at "girl things" today (and some boys are tempted to apply this to things as innocuous as writing, reading, or giving affection to a parent) finds it that much easier to look down his nose at romance, affection, and being a nuturing parent later because they too are "girl things" that somehow offend his false sense of masculinity. The same is true for girls.

It is possible to go too far with this, of course, and try to force boys to play with dolls and force girls to play contact sports — even when they have zero interest in such activities — in an effort to aggressively discourage the "stereotyping of roles." I am not advocating this completely absurd parenting strategy. What I am saying, though, is that a girl who likes to climb trees and play contact sports, or a boy who happens to have an attachment to a My Buddy or Cabbage Patch doll (or the like) should never, ever be treated by a parent or a friend in a way that makes them question their God-given femininity or masculinity.

There is nothing wrong with boys preferring to play with boys and girls preferring to play with girls at this age, but we must discourage our children from viewing with disdain the things that their friends, brothers, or sisters value. When we see this behavior, we should simply say, "It's okay that you don't like to do (such and such) but it is something that (s)he likes. That is the way God made him/her, and we must be respectful of those differences. Please apologize for your rudeness."

6. Encourage good relationships between brothers and sisters.

The relationship between brothers and sisters affects future marital relationships almost as much as the modeling of the parents does. The Holy Father, in "The Gospel of Life," encourages families to exhibit "a respect for others, a sense of justice, cordial openness, dialogue, generous service, solidarity, and all the other values which help us live life as a gift." Foster these virtues in your family, especially in the interactions between your sons and daughters. Do whatever is possible to discourage bickering and increase effective problem-solving between siblings.

7. Pray about the meaning of the body.

Pope John Paul II encourages all Christians to pray to understand the meaning and the gift of their physical body. The Psalmist praises God saying, "fearful and wonderful . . . are thy works" (Ps 139:14). How has God made you? What gifts has God given you as a person? What gifts has God given you as a man/woman? What unique skills, talents, and sensitivities do you have? Encourage your children — by your own example — to discern the answers to these questions for themselves. Then encourage your children to celebrate the answers to those questions in their daily life, so that they will be living, breathing examples of Christian man-/womanhood.

Handling early questions about sex

According to *The Truth and Meaning of Human Sexuality*, children of this age are often uninterested and even appropriately oblivious to sexual issues. This is generally true. The only exceptions to this rule are those questions about sex that may arise as the result of natural curiosity at the birth of brothers or sisters, for example, or questions that may come up owing to an unfortunate exposure to sexual situations in the media.

For more information on promoting what I call "sibling revelry" (the antithesis of "sibling rivalry") see *Parenting with Grace* or contact the Pastoral Solutions Institute (740-266-6461; http://www.exceptional marriages.com).

When answering your child's basic questions about sex and procreation at this stage, it is best to give simple, innocent answers, keeping in mind to always provide the information you are giving in a moral and spiritual context. The best way I have found to explain sex to a child of this age is to say something like the following:

When a man and a woman are ready to have children, God lets them share a special hug that He invented, where all the parts of the man and all the parts of the woman fit together in a beautiful way so they can make a baby. You can't have a baby from just a regular hug, like the kind mom, dad, your brothers, sisters, or friends give you. But only from those special hugs that allow husbands and wives to be mommies and daddies.

Usually this is a sufficient answer at this stage of the game, but as always, you will want to let your child take the lead in asking further questions, always making sure that your answers are simple, honest, faithful, and friendly.

One question that may come up as the result of your child's meeting someone who has a child and is not married is, "I thought you had to be married to have babies." I have found that the best way to handle this question is with the following:

Well, men and women who aren't married sometimes try to do that special hug on their own, because they think it would be fun. But when men and women do that, it increases the chances that their baby will grow up in a home without a daddy, because daddies who aren't married often run away from mommies after their babies are born, and that makes God, the mommies, and the babies very sad.

If your child then asks, "Why do some daddies do that?" You might respond by saying, "*I don't know, honey. But sometimes people make sad and foolish choices and that makes God very sad. Can you promise me that you will never do that hug unless you are married so that your babies will always have a daddy and God will be happy with you?"*

If your child sees something inappropriate on television or in a magazine and asks you a question about it, the first thing you need to do is remain calm. Ask the child what she thinks it is that she saw, and what it means to her first. Then, if you feel it is appropriate, tell your child what you think she needs to know, always remembering to be gentle and to connect what you tell the child to the greater, positive, spiritual context.

Likewise, at this stage of the game, it is sometimes all right to let some innocent misperceptions stand. For example, if your child comes to you giggling and says, "I saw a boy and a girl wrestling on TV with no clothes!" This may or may not be the time to introduce your child to the "hug talk." You will have to use your own discretion of course, but in many instances, it would be enough to matter-of-factly say, "Really? Hmm. Do you think that was very modest of them to be playing with no clothes, on television no less?" Child giggles, "No way." You respond innocently, "Let's not watch that channel anymore. I don't think I like those shows."

Set appropriate but gentle limits around masturbatory activity

For most children this will not be a problem, but sometimes, especially in times of stress or boredom, children of this age will touch themselves in inappropriate ways. If your child is doing this, and simple redirection (like "Please don't do that, honey.") isn't working, it might be time to give a more thorough explanation of the feelings that accompany self-touching.

First, give your child the "hug talk" I outlined in an earlier section of this chapter. Then explain that the feelings the child is getting from touching him- or herself are part of that special hug. Not all of it, but part of it. (This is so your child doesn't think he or she can become pregnant from masturbating. There are many problems associated with this behavior, but fortunately, pregnancy isn't one of them.) Tell your child that when he or she tries to make those feelings him- or herself, it is like telling God that he or she is ready to have a baby and God knows that he or she is not ready to have a baby. So touching him- or herself like that is kind of like lying to God, and that makes God feel sad. Now, God knows he or she didn't mean to lie, so God isn't angry at your child, but now that your child understands what those feelings mean, God will be very sad if your child does it again.

Depending upon whether or not you think it appropriate, you might also let your child know that sometimes, people who touch themselves like that grow to like those feelings even more than they like babies, and so they grow up not caring about the babies they make. Since you don't want your children to ever be so selfish, they need to make good choices now and stop touching themselves that way.

Again, you will need to decide how much information the situation calls for and exactly how you want to share that information. But I offer the above as an example of one way to faithfully explain the morality of what your child is doing without becoming some screaming, shrieking idiot and making your child ashamed of his or her sexuality in the process. By taking such a sensitive, faithful, and direct approach, you do nothing to undermine the inherent goodness of sexuality, but at the same time you take steps to keep sexuality in its place.

So far, we've just been warming up. In the next chapter, we'll take on puberty. Buckle your seatbelts, folks; the ride's about to get interesting!

CHAPTER SIX

The Apprenticeship Years

Puberty (Ages 10-14)

Puberty . . . is a time in which parents are called to be particularly attentive to the Christian education of their children. . . . Parents should pay particular attention to their children's gradual physical development and to their physical and psychological changes. . . .Without showing anxiety, fear, or obsessive concern, parents will not let cowardice or convenience hinder their work. This is naturally an important moment in teaching the value of chastity, which will also be expressed in the way sexual information is given. In this phase, educational needs also concern the genital aspects, hence requiring a presentation both on the level of values and the reality as a whole. Moreover, this implies an understanding of the context of procreation, marriage, and the family, which must be kept present in an authentic task of sexual education.

~The Pontifical Council on the Family,
The Truth and Meaning of Human Sexuality

Up until now, most of our work has been about pouring a foundation for a healthy sexuality and then allowing that foundation to "set up." From this point on, however, we will begin building the structure that rests on that foundation.

Usually referring to the ages between ten and fourteen, puberty is the time when sexual education deals more specifically with genital and reproductive issues which are being raised as the child is experiencing physical maturation. Some of the major parenting tasks include the following:

- Educating the pre-teen/early teen about changes occurring in his or her body.
- Educating the young person about the basic biology of sex and reproduction, including some basic information about Natural Family Planning.
- Initiating basic discussions about identity and how the young person can find his/her place in the world.
- Discussing sexual feelings and the appropriate ways to manage them.
- Learning how to build friendships with members of the opposite sex.
- Setting appropriate rules for dealing with the opposite sex.
- Promoting a positive connection with the Church and a practical, personal experience of God.

We will spend the rest of this chapter examining each of the above more closely.

Educating the pre-teen/early teen about changes occurring in his or her body

Phillip, a phone client of mine, recently shared the following story.

"When I was about 13, my nipples started hurting when I dried myself getting out of the shower. It was uncomfortable and I was embarrassed, so I didn't say anything about the pain. I just kept checking myself in the mirror to see if I could see something.

"I remember one day looking in the mirror and seeing something that terrified me. My chest was getting bigger. Of course, what was happening was that I was getting some normal definition to my chest, but I didn't know that then. I was sure that I was growing breasts!

"I was always kind of a sensitive kid, and I got teased a lot for being a 'sissy' when I was in grade school. Now I was afraid that I was going to look like a girl too. I remember begging God not to let me grow breasts. I didn't want to look like a girl and have the 'man-boobies' that I overheard a late-night comedian talking about.

"After checking myself in the mirror three times a day for a month, the pain stopped and my chest stopped growing. Only then did I figure out for myself that this must be one of those 'guy things,' like hair under my arms. But I remember that being one of the worst four weeks of my adolescence."

"I don't think any of us were prepared for what was happening," said Anna. *"I got the whole talk. I was expecting breasts (never happened, sorry to say) and even my period. But when my mom told me about my period, she never said anything about blood. She just said it was 'a wonderful and magical thing that happens when a young girl is becoming a woman.'*

"Well, one day I was in school when I got such terrible cramps, I thought I was going to die. I went to the nurse's station and my mom came to get me. When I got home and changed into my pajamas, blood gushed everywhere. I was terrified. I thought I was hemor-

rhaging. My mother said, 'Oh, honey! Mazel Tov! My little girl became a woman.'

"*I just looked at her in terror and screamed. 'I'm never going to be a woman. I'm bleeding to death!' *"

———————

Puberty can be a frightening time for a young man or woman. It is the time when you feel like your body is being taken over by aliens. Strange things are happening, you feel like a freak, and it is all you can do to keep at least a veneer of coolness about you.

No matter what we tell our children, nothing will be able to completely prepare them for what they are going to go through over the next few years. Even so, it will be important for us to do as much as we can to be sensitive to their changing bodies, and prepare them for those changes as soon as possible, so that they have the information when they need it. The following are some ways you can help make this transition easier for your children.

1. Give them what they need to care for their bodies.

One of the first things you will need to do to help your child cope with puberty is to prepare him or her for the changes in hygiene that are required of a growing boy or girl. This is often the first time children need deodorant, for example, or the first time they will be expected to shower after gym class at school.

One day, around the age that a young man or woman might begin needing such things (but preferably before the need has become embarrassingly obvious), give your son or daughter a gift package of scented soaps, deodorant, feminine products for your young woman, and colognes or perfumes, and tell your youths how to use them properly, specifically, that they need to use enough to keep themselves clean and fresh-smelling, but not so much that they will gag the people around them.

I would also recommend writing a letter to your son or daughter, telling the young person how proud you are of who he or she is becoming so far, and of how pleased you are that he or she is becoming more and more of an adult every day. In the letter, let your child know, without going into great detail (details should be reserved for one-to-one talks) about the changes that he or she will be going through, and that you want to work harder than ever to be present as he or she learns what it means to become a man or woman. Invite your youth to ask you questions. Wherever possible, I would recommend that both the mother and the father write separate letters that offer their love, and the unique perspectives and support they can bring to the next few years of the young person's life. Generally speaking, the same-sex parent will be taking the lead over the next few years for giving guidance on the changes that are happening, but the opposite-sex parent should not excuse him- or herself from all of the proceedings. Both parents have valuable and unique information to share with their child and should make themselves available to provide counsel whenever their child needs it.

2. Help the child cope with embarrassment and awkwardness.

This is the time when your young men and women are comparing themselves to other young men and women. Be prepared to help your son deal with the fact that he has to shower in front of other boys at school who have more hair than he does or who are otherwise more developed than he is. Be aware that your daughter may be concerned that her breasts are developing too much or too slowly, or that she is not getting her period as soon as the other girls in her class.

This would be a good time to initiate regular talks with your child about what these years were like for you. Find photographs of yourself that show your own development from child to adult. Also, to aid your discussion, take some time to complete the following exercise. Write your answers on a separate sheet of paper and keep it for your own reference.

a. *What do you remember as being the most difficult times about puberty? How did you deal with your changing body? Showering as a group? Comparing your breasts to other girls? Comparing penis size or hair growth at the urinal? Acne? Body odor?*

b. *How did you respond to your first period, or wet dream?*

c. *When did you start having your first sexual attractions? What do you wish you had known then about those feelings? What was the most useful thing you were ever taught or learned about keeping sexual feelings respectfully in check?*

d. *What do you wish a sensitive adult had told you about the changes you went through from ages 10 to 14? How do you wish the adults in your life had acted toward you? (For example, did they call unnecessary attention to your bodily changes, or tease you in some way that was hurtful? Or did they not give you enough information, or not respond to your questions, or ignore the changes you were going through?)*

Writing out thoughtful and thorough answers to the above questions will help you get in touch with some of the things to look for in your own young person's life and recall the things that you wish others had done to prepare you for puberty. While I would not suggest that you simply write answers to these questions and hand your child the paper, I would suggest that you prepare yourself to share as much about your own experiences as you can when the time presents itself. You are your child's teacher in these matters. You must be willing to find a way to use your experiences to enlighten your child. Become comfortable with those experiences and find respectful ways to communicate them to your child.

3. Look for indirect signs that your child needs some guidance.

It is not unusual for a child of this age to become somewhat secretive with regard to the changes he or she is experiencing in his or her body and not ask questions even when it is important to do so. Don't be surprised if this happens no matter how many times you tell your child, "Don't be afraid to tell me anything or ask me anything anytime." Such comments have the effect of letting a parent off the hook without ever having to really do anything. In fact, it's a bit like saying to a person who has lost a spouse, "Let me know if I can do anything." Such expressions are polite and sincere enough, but they lack a certain commitment.

In addition to giving verbal encouragement to your child, you will need to look for the indirect signs your child may be giving you that indicate a need for your counsel. Have you noticed some stains when you change your son's bed sheets? Perhaps this would be a good time to initiate a discussion about wet dreams or, if it is a more frequent occurrence, masturbation. Is your daughter withdrawing from friends? Perhaps this is a good time to ask some gentle questions, including questions about whether she ever compares herself to the other girls in class. Is your child beginning to spend an inordinate amount of time in the bathroom? Maybe it's time to do some gentle probing about the changes your youth is noticing in his or her body, or give some instruction in hygiene.

Be sensitive to your children's privacy, but use the nonverbal signs to guide you about when you should initiate discussions concerning bodily changes, sexuality, or feelings for the opposite sex.

Educating the young person about the basic biology of sex and reproduction, including some basic information about NFP

At this time, you will need to give more thorough information about sex, procreation, and marriage, as well as the spiritual meaning of it all.

Presumably, by now your child already knows about the "special hug" I described in the last chapter on middle childhood. Now is the time to fill in some of the blanks. For example, previously, your child knew that the special hug was one in which all the parts of the man fit together with all the parts of the woman in a special way, so that they could make a baby (for a more thorough explanation of "the hug talk" please refer to the last chapter). Now it will be time to more specifically define those parts and the "gifts" a man and woman give each other to make a baby.

God gives a husband and wife special gifts to give each other when they share that special hug where all the husband's parts, especially his penis, fit into all the wife's parts, especially her vagina.

The man gives his wife a gift called "sperm," which God has given him to make a baby. And the woman gives her husband a gift called an "ovum" (egg), which God has given her to make a baby. God then puts the egg and the sperm together — like two pieces of a very special puzzle — inside the wife's body and carries the brand

new baby (who is now so small you can't even see him — but God can)
to a special place called the uterus. That's a place inside the woman
that God made just for the baby, and belongs to the baby — it's like
the baby's first room. The baby snuggles up inside the special room
God made for him, and God feeds him with special food for nine
months until he grows big and strong. Then, when it's time for his
birthday, God carefully pushes the baby out of the mom, through her
vagina, and into her arms, so that she can nurse him and cuddle him,
and keep him safe for God.

I like this explanation because it is honest, innocent, brings
God into the picture, and uses language that subtly opposes
the pro-abortion slogan "My body, my choice." I would not
suggest sitting down and giving the above as "the talk." Rather,
I present the above to you as a guide that you can follow, adapt
to your needs, and reveal to your child in bits and pieces at the
times and in the stages you see fit. With regard to this last
point, however, I would recommend that you reveal just about
all of the above information at least by the time your child is in
fifth or sixth grade — especially if he or she attends "away
school" as opposed to being home-schooled — because if you
wait any longer, you run the risk of showing up second, after
your child's peers, for your child's sexual education. The only
way such an honest and innocent explanation of sex and reproduction as the above will "take" for your child is if you get
there first.

In addition to the above, once your daughter has begun men-
struating, or your son is showing signs that he is beginning to
mature sexually, I would recommend giving some basic information about Natural Family Planning. I would not necessarily
talk about NFP as a method of achieving or avoiding pregnancy,
but I would suggest teaching your daughter to chart her cycles
as a way of getting to know the miracle that is going on inside

her body and how God is making so much happen in her without her even knowing it. Also, you should show it as the way God, through the Church, has given a woman to monitor her health and know her body. Likewise, if the mother is teaching her daughter how to chart her cycles, then the mother (and through the mother, the father) will be more aware of, and more sensitive to, the emotional shifts the daughter is experiencing.

Boys usually begin maturing sexually later than girls, so they will not need to encounter NFP quite as early as their sisters, but at the time that your young men begin maturing and, by inference, making sperm (usually anywhere between twelve and fourteen), you are obliged to teach them about the responsibility that accompanies the gift God is giving them. As the saying goes, "From those to whom much is given, much will be required."

Explain to your sons that as God is giving them the gift of their sexuality, He is asking them to spend the next several years learning how to use that gift properly. Part of that means that if he marries, he will be responsible for working with his wife to determine God's will for their lives, including when to have children and how many children to have. These are decisions that need to be made every month in collaboration with his wife and with prayer. After he is married, part of his responsibility will be to help his wife do something called charting, which means that he will write down the different signs that tell how healthy his wife is and when they could have a baby.

I am aware of some families where the brother may chart his sister's temperatures for her, or even some cases where the mother shares her own NFP chart (minus the coitus record, of course) with the intent of acquainting the young men and women of the house with NFP. I also know some families who object to this idea on privacy or modesty grounds. You will have to decide whether having boys record their sister's or mother's temperatures is an option for your family, but as long as the person whose chart it is (the mother or sister) is not terribly opposed to the idea (you really have to respect her opinion on this), I feel favorably toward the idea because it decreases the chances that your young teens will eroticize their sexuality. Treated in this manner, you are more likely to present this kind of information as a literal fact of life as opposed to some glamorous, dangerous, erotic mystery. Nevertheless, I leave the final decision to your prayerful discretion.

Whether or not you decide to enlist your pubescent boys in the charting process, they can begin doing the other thing needed for a healthy marital sexuality. They can pray. In fact, your daughters should do this too.

Every morning, encourage your sons and your daughters to say the following prayer, or one similar to it, the first thing after they open their eyes.

Lord, help me to know your will for my life.

If you want me to marry, then bless the boy/girl you have already chosen for me and help him/her to draw closer to you every day. Lead me to love you more every day too, and help me to keep myself a pure gift for my future husband/wife. And until that time, teach me all the things I need to know to be the husband/wife you would want me to be.

Additionally, encourage a devotion to St. Joseph for your boys and a devotion to the Blessed Mother for your girls. Instruct them to regularly ask the Holy Family to pray for them.

The Christian who wants to have a healthy sexuality needs to have a good sense of spiritual discernment, before and after marriage. The only way to develop this specific kind of discernment is to constantly bring one's sexual self before God for instruction, nurturing, and guidance. Teaching your children to do this from the earliest stages of their sexual maturation will increase the chances that they will develop a healthy and holy sexuality.

Initiating basic discussions about identity and how the young person can find his place in the world

Your child is beginning to enter a stage of development where he is going to begin searching for his unique identity. If you do not give him (or her) the tools to foster this identity, then he/she is more likely seek out his/her identity through inappropriate actions, such as promiscuity, drug abuse, criminal activity, or other high-risk behaviors.

Studies consistently show that children who are passionately committed to various hobbies and extracurricular activities tend to be less likely to engage in risk-taking behavior, including premarital sex. Now is the time to get your child involved in various group activities, to foster his/her interests and hobbies, to show him or her that life is much more than dating and scoping out cute members of the opposite sex.

Beyond encouraging your young person to get involved, you will want to help him solidify what I call a personal mission statement. That is, what qualities does he wish to be known for at the end of his life and what choices does he have to start making, today, in order to eventually achieve those qualities.

Discussing sexual feelings and the appropriate ways to manage them

As parents, we cannot be intimidated by the sexual feelings our children are beginning to have at this age. We must be prepared to teach our children what God's purpose behind sexual feelings are.

You might say that the purpose of those sexual feelings is to prepare young people for marriage, to encourage them to begin praying for their future partner. Of course, this is absolutely correct — and when they have those feelings, they should do exactly that — but there is an even more basic meaning to feelings of sexual attraction, a meaning that applies even to those young people considering priestly or religious life.

In light of Pope John Paul's "Theology of the Body," it becomes possible to see that sexual attraction gives strong evidence of the donative meaning of the body. That is to say, sexual attraction is God's way of reminding us that we were not created for ourselves, that we were ultimately created to give ourselves to others, to work for their good. For those who marry, that gift of self can have a genital dimension, but for everyone — including those who are called to a celibate, religious life — sexuality and sexual attraction have a deeper meaning. It is God's way of calling us to remember that we cannot live for ourselves, and whether we marry or not, we are to use our bodies to work for the good of others.

Teach your children from this age forward that sexual attraction, in its purest form, is really the voice of God calling us to pray, or do some genuine act of service, for the person who has come to our attention. While it is true that men and women can pervert and distort God's intended use of sexual feelings by allowing them

I discuss this process in much more detail in *Parenting with Grace*. If you are interested in learning more about how to teach this skill to your teen I recommend that resource, as well as the book *Seven Habits of Highly Effective Teens* which is written by Stephen Covey's son and applies his principles to adolescent life.

to objectify others, it does not change the fact that when God originally created man and woman and gave them those feelings, He intended those feelings to be used in a way that called the man and woman, indeed all people, to work for one another's good.

Cynical readers might be led to say that the above advice is not very practical. How, for instance, does this help a young person deal with pent-up sexual frustration and other inappropriate levels of sexual excitement? It works like this. Cognitive psychologists have discovered that feelings are created by the thoughts we think about the circumstances in which we find ourselves. For instance, you and I could share exactly the same experience — say, a symphony — but feel entirely different about that experience (for example, I may love it while you may hate it), simply because inside our heads we are telling ourselves different things about the experience. In the above example, while I am sitting in the concert hall, I am saying things in my head like, "This is beautiful. Listen to all the layers of sound. How amazing it is to watch all of the musicians play in perfect synch with each other. This piece reminds me of . . . ." At the same time, you may be sitting next to me saying to yourself, "I would rather be anywhere but here. What time is it? I'm so bored. I'm sooooooo bored. I . . . . am . . . . so . . . . b . . . o . . . r . . . e . . . d . . . ! I . . . am . . . so . . . zzzzzzzzzzz."

To sum up, the reason I am enjoying myself and you are not is that each of us is putting a different "spin" on the experience in our own minds, and those thoughts are actually creating our feelings. Now to the subject at hand.

If every time I am attracted to a woman, especially my wife, I say to myself, "What a hot babe. I would love to get into her pants," I am actually cultivating feelings of lust. I am nursing those feelings of sexual attraction for my own benefit and speaking of the other person as if she were an object that I could pose and use as I saw fit. On the other hand, if I experience sexual attraction and say in my mind, "Thank You, God, for creating this person and giving her Your beauty. Bless her," I will actually experience feelings of altruism because of the initial sexual attraction.

Some of you may think this is absurd, but it is not. Neither does it require heroic virtue to do. Patience and commitment? Yes. Heroism? Absolutely not. If I can regularly and reasonably expect persons who are consumed by depression or panic attacks to change their thought processes and thereby create new and healthier feeling states, why is it any less reasonable for us to expect ourselves, each other, and our children to mind their thoughts so that they do not become lustful? In fact, this is exactly what Jesus commands us to do when he tells us, "I say to you that anyone who looks at a woman lustfully has already committed adultery." Jesus, the Son of God, knew exactly why the Father gave us feelings of sexual attraction. It was not to give us something pleasant to think about when we are bored. It was to remind us to pray for the person He is calling to our attention and, when possible, do something, however small, to make that person's life easier or more pleasant.

Teach your children the true meaning of sexual attraction, and you will be giving them them a leg up in the struggle to remain chaste up to and even after marriage.

Learning how to build friendships with members of the opposite sex

The adult who is capable of a healthy romantic, sexual, marital relationship has passed through three stages in his or her relationship to others. First, he or she has learned to be friends with people of his or her own gender. Second, he or she has learned how to have platonic friendships with members of the opposite sex. Third, he or she has learned how to maintain the primacy of friendship even when mutual romantic feelings are involved. Finally, he or she is ready to celebrate a lifelong friendship with one special person that is largely sexual in nature.

Middle and late childhood is the time in which a child learns the basics of being a good friend to those of his own gender. Puberty is the time of life when the young person should be encouraged to apply these same rules to friendships with members of the opposite sex.

Because of strong cultural influences, many children, and even their parents, tend to skip over this stage of psychosexual development and rush right into the quasi-dating phase. This is a tragic mistake, not because there is anything wrong with romantic feelings, but because encouraging those feelings in pre-adolescents and young adolescents — even more than they already exist — leads to children who are trying to grow up too fast. These children end up losing themselves in romantic relationships long before they have ever had a chance to develop a sense of self or the ability to befriend a member of the opposite sex.

Instead, the wise parent encourages young men and women at this age to associate in groups that include members of the opposite sex. This is important because boys and girls have different ways of approaching life, and by learning to befriend each other, they learn to understand each other's "languages" (attitudes and approaches to life) so that when they eventually do marry, they don't stand around looking at their partner saying, "(Wo)Men! Who can understand 'em?"

I would also suggest that, while parents do not wish to give the impression of breathing down their youth's neck, it is advisable to provide appropriate levels of supervision to these mixed-gender gatherings just in case things go occasionally awry. Inevitably, some feelings of affection, requited or otherwise, may enter into the group — and your child, or his friends, will need a thoughtful, respectful parent to bounce ideas off of. The fact is, young people of this age — indeed, young people of any age — often go looking for sensitive adults to serve as sounding boards. The reason so many of these sought-after adults are not the child's parents is that many times the parent is more interested in being right than in being helpful. I do not mean to imply that parents should not be prepared to lay down the law with their children — quite the opposite. Rather, I mean that even more important than being right in the presence of our children, we need to give our children the skills to decide to the right thing on their own. An important prerequisite to doing this is being a good listener.

While we are on the subject of relating to the opposite sex, many parents ask me how old their children should be before they are allowed to date. Within certain limits, I really don't consider this so much a question of age as it is a question of skill. I would suggest that your teen is too young to date until he or she has demonstrated the ability to have basically platonic friendships with several members of the opposite sex. Some youths learn this skill at 14 or 15 (rarely, if ever, before); some don't learn it until they are 43 and working on their second marriage, but the answer remains the same. Don't rush the dating question. Set up, or at least encourage, your teen to enlist in situations where your child can freely associate with peers of the same and opposite sex. Once he or she has demonstrated the ability to relate in a sane, friendly way to the young men and women in the group, he or she can be said to have the maturity required to be given at least some limited dating privileges which are entirely at your discretion.

We will talk more about dating, boyfriends, and girl friends in the next section on adolescence, but since many first-dating questions arise in late puberty (age 14 or so), I want to take a few moments here to give you some additional guidance on the topic — because, as far as first love goes, nothing is more intoxicating, or for the parent, more terrifying. Even the sanest grown-ups among us will catch themselves thinking, *"What if my baby falls in love with someone named 'Slash' and they run away together to join a coven?"* Admit it. You've thought it. I know you have.

Let me reassure you. Most likely this nightmare will remain a dark figment of your parental imagination. But in case you're still nervous, consider the following tips for surviving the early dating years.

1. Set Your Limits.

An important part of your role in supporting and educating your young teen is setting boundaries. While no one can tell you exactly where to draw the lines, some issues you might want to address include the following: Has your teen demonstrated an ability to befriend members of the opposite sex (a possible indicator of readiness to be given some limited dating privileges)? How will you get to know your child's date? Where should they be allowed to go? Is dating in a group preferable to going as a couple? (This is always true for younger teens.) Under what conditions must they call you? How do you expect your teen to treat his/her date? What expectations should (s)he have about the way (s)he should be treated by the date? What should they do in case of emergency? What time should they be back?

Your teen may not necessarily enjoy addressing such questions (and perhaps neither will you), but you are well within your rights and responsibilities as a parent to require the discussion anyway. Likewise, I would suggest that you have the right to require your teen to respond to those questions respectfully and attentively before gaining permission to go on the date, on the grounds that dating requires a certain maturity — and if they can't express that maturity with you, you may be right to question the level of maturity he or she will exhibit on a date. At the same time, you would do well not to be too heavy-handed in your approach. After all, this is not an interrogation. It is a friendly meeting between a teacher and student, the purpose of which is to discuss, openly and respectfully, an important stage of life. Adopting this respectful, helpful, but firm attitude toward your teen, and requiring a similar attitude in response, will help you maintain your rapport with your child, and train him or her up properly as (s)he becomes a young man or woman.

2. "Puppy Love" Is Important. Please, Don't Tease.

As a way of dealing with our anxiety over our children's growing up, we often tease them about their relationships. Worse, we waste a lot of air lecturing them on how unimportant "this dating stuff" is. All we end up doing, of course, is alienating our kids. People don't like to have their concerns minimized, or their needs poked fun at, and teen-agers are especially sensitive to this. Engaging in too much of even the most good-natured kidding may eventually leave us wondering, "Why won't he talk to me anymore?"

As parents, we must remember that "puppy-love relationships" are important, not just because our kids think they are, but because they serve an essential developmental function. They help our adolescents learn about themselves — their likes and dislikes, their strengths and weaknesses; in short, who they want to be when they grow up. Martin Buber said, "To be is to be in relation to others." Your children are going to test this motto out to the max. Over the next few years, they will make friends with and date a wide — and sometimes strange — variety of people to help them clarify their own dreams, goals, and values. Your ability to be respectful of your teens' dating relationships will be the best way to encourage their willingness to confide in you and receive guidance from you.

3. Encourage Your Child's Well-Roundedness.

Let's face it, even the healthiest teen can get a little obsessive about a boyfriend or girl friend from time to time. Though this is fairly normal, it is not desirable, and we need to help our kids through it. What to do?

I find the best way to solve this problem is to spend much more time encouraging their involvement in other friendships, hobbies, community, church, or extracurricular activities than discouraging the importance of their love life. On the one hand, this approach benefits the parent because a busy kid has fewer opportunities to make stupid choices. On the other hand, it benefits your children because they will have more than just their relationship to live for. This enables teens to be more discriminating both about whom they go out with and what they do while they are out. Ideally, you want to get your kids hooked into these activities while they are still pre-teens, but one way or another, the solution for the problem of love-struck adolescents remains *increasing the variety of opportunities to socialize*, not merely decreasing the social outlet they are obsessed with.

4. Foster Your Own Relationship With Your Teen.

You want to give your teen advice, but your advice will not be accepted unless you have rapport with her, and the only way to maintain rapport is to spend time doing things together. Those coveted parent/child heart-to-hearts don't occur simply because they should; they occur when you least expect it —

while you are doing yard work together, working on the car, hiking, going to concerts, anything. Adolescents don't do well with structured "Let's share time," but they will open up, on their own terms, while engaged in some innocuous activity with a caring parent. Now, more than ever, your adolescent needs you to put in the time. Your effort will be rewarded with their confidence.

5. Give Them the Tools to Find Their Own Healthy Answers.

No matter how cool we are as parents, sometimes our kids will not come to us with their concerns. But this does not mean we cannot still influence their choices. More important than supplying young Romeos and Juliets with answers is teaching them how to find the healthiest answers on their own. Books like Mary Beth Bonacci's *Real Love* are essential resources for the hapless parent of a lovestruck teen. Give your sons or daughters a book like this as a "just-because" present with a letter that tells them how proud you are of the young men or women they are becoming. Alternatively, if you or your child aren't into "mushy stuff," simply leave the book in an obvious place (like on the toilet tank) where it can be consulted in privacy. Either way you will be giving your young persons an important message, that you support them in this exciting time of their lives *and* you care enough to give them the tools they need to make healthy choices.

6. Take Stock of Your Marriage.

Your young teens would be loath to admit it, but your marriage is going to be their special teacher over the next few years. They will be especially interested in how you and your mate deal with affection, conflict, and finding the balance between work, personal interests, and home life. Take a cue from your kid. Use this time to get back in touch with your mate. Work on your romantic side. Develop deeper intimacy with your spouse. Show your kids what to expect — no, what to *demand* — from a relationship, not just what to settle for.

In short, be calm, be available, be encouraging, be a good model, and most of all, be on your way. After all, little Margaret Mary (or John Paul) is waiting at the Cine-Plex for you-know-who.

Setting appropriate rules for dealing with the opposite sex

Closely associated with encouraging your children to build friendships with members of the opposite sex and, in late puberty/early adolescence, allowing some limited dating privileges, is setting appropriate rules for conduct. While we talked about some of the questions you should settle before your teen begins dating, the following are more general rules for dealing with the opposite sex.

1. Encourage Modesty in Thought, Action, and Dress.

Modesty is not a virtue of repression. Likewise, nowhere in the *Catechism of the Catholic Church* does it say that in order to be modest, we must require our daughters (or our wives for that matter) to wear shapeless denim jumpers. To the contrary, modesty is a virtue that, according to Father Peter Stravinkas in the *Catholic Encyclopedia (revised edition)*, facilitates good relations and communication by causing us to avoid over-the-top behavior, including overly fussy manners and outrageous styles of dress (e.g., "Look at how sexy/wealthy/*au courant* I am!") or even over-the-top displays of piety ("Look at how piously dumpy I am!").

Modesty is the virtue that prevents us from making other people uncomfortable by our presence. It gives us the ability to avoid presenting ourselves either as objects (of ridicule or titillation) or freaks. It permits us to live the "attractive faith" St. Francis de Sales called us to exhibit when he encouraged Christians to be "the most attractive people in the room, barring frivolity" (cf. *Introduction to the Devout Life*).

So we see that even though modesty is, in part, about hem- and necklines, this is the most basic and most arbitrary form of it. Really, modesty is about sensitivity. A sensitivity to the image I am projecting, to the comfort level (or moral level) of the people I am associating with, to the etiquette required of me by the situations in which I find myself. All for the purpose of displaying an "attractive faith." If the way I am behaving, speaking, or dressing either is unattractive or obscures the faith I am trying to live out (by making me appear either too erotic or too freakish), then it is immodest.

If you teach your children good manners in general, as well as a sensitivity to their surroundings, you will raise teens to whom modesty in dress comes fairly naturally (with perhaps some occasional guidance). But if you fail to train your child in proper manners and sensitivity to her surroundings and instead focus on becoming the fashion police, you will end up with a teen who dresses like something out of your worst nightmare. A teen who, as soon as she leaves the house, will ditch the denim jumper you foisted upon her and slip on the micro-miniskirt stashed in her gym bag.

When it comes to encouraging modesty in thought, this means teaching your children not to treat, or even think of, other people as objects for their amusement. Regardless of how another person dresses, it is not your job or your children's job to think lewd thoughts or even judgmental thoughts about them. To do so is immodest. If you must think anything about a person who offends your sense of style or modesty, then you should think, "Lord, help me see and treat that person with respect." Model and teach this attitude to your children and you will be on your way to fostering a modest spirit in yourself and your teens.

2. Encourage Respect and Helpfulness.

Keeping in mind that, as far as Catholic Christians are concerned, the entire point of relationships is to work for the good of another, we need to encourage our children to develop helpful and respectful attitudes toward everyone, but especially members of the opposite sex. Teach your children the importance of listening to their friends, of performing little acts of kindness (like holding doors, speaking respectfully, and asking relevant questions, carrying books, getting assignments for sick friends), not to be rewarded in any way, but because it is the right thing to do. Give examples of those acts of kindness, and model those actions in your own marriage.

3. Remember That Friendship Comes First.

Teach your children that friendship is the most important part of a relationship between two people — especially people of the opposite sex — and that true friends are people who make you freer to be the person God created you to be. If a person makes you feel embarrassed to exercise your talents, express your opinions, or share your thoughts, that person is not a friend, and your teens would be better off putting a respectful distance between themselves and that person, whether that person is of the same or the opposite sex.

Once your teen understands this definition of friends (over the more common definition of "someone with whom I hang out"), continue to remind her that she must try never to do any-thing to offend the respect and encouragement that stands at the heart of friendship, nor should she tolerate anyone else offering her anything less than that same respect and encouragement. Of course, you must give your child the skills to negotiate these conflicts (preferably by modeling them in your own marriage), but you must first give your child the ability to set respectful limits for her own behavior toward others, as well as the ability to draw respectful lines in the sand when someone else tries to trample her God-given dignity.

Let the above three rules serve as the basis for teaching your children about befriending the opposite sex and you will be pleasantly surprised at both the quality and chastity of your teens' relationships

Promoting a positive connection with the Church and a practical, personal experience of God

All of the information in this book will be utterly useless to you if you do not find some way to help your teen connect on a personal, emotional level with his or her faith. It is such a con-nection to the faith, and this connection alone, that will give your young person the will to be chaste, modest, and moral when his or her peers are acting to the contrary — and you are not looking.

A woman recently called me to complain that her daughter was rejecting the faith. *"She was always so compliant. She has gone to Catholic school all her life and never gave us any trouble about going to church. Now, all of a sudden, she thinks it is all irrelevant and she fights with us. I don't know what to do."*

While it is perfectly natural for teens to begin asking hard questions about the beliefs they had always accepted as fact because their parents told them it was so, there are some dangers involved in the questioning process. The best way to keep a child from losing his or her faith through this time of questioning is to foster a strong, personal, and emotional faith in the child in addition to any catechesis he or she is receiving. While an emotional faith, the kind that is evident in things like the Charismatic movement, Life Teen, the nationwide Franciscan University Youth Conferences, and World Youth Days, is hardly the most mature variety of faith, it is an important aspect of everyone's faith experience nonetheless and must be fostered. The fact is, before God can capture our minds, He must be the master of our hearts. It is this combination that leads to what has been called "dynamic orthodoxy." (Compare this to those so-called "orthodox" individuals who might better be described as "grimly pious.")

The problem is, too many children ride on the coattails of their parents' faith and morals. They go to church and learn about the faith because they have to, and they have not yet found the voice to challenge their parents' authority in these matters. Their parents, on the other hand, make the tragic mistake of assuming that compliance and faith are the same thing, only to discover in adolescence that, *SURPRISE*, they are not.

The best way to help a young teen hold onto his or her faith and morals, even while he or she is intellectually questioning the very roots of those things, is to first model your love for Christ and his Church, and then give your child myriad opportunities to fall head over heels in love with Christ. All the education on chastity in the world will not benefit your child if you have not fostered a personal commitment to the faith in your child as evidenced by an expressive, emotional, head-over-heels-in-love-with-Jesus attitude.

Conclusion

While we have not covered everything that needs to be said about helping your child successfully negotiate the physical, emotional, and social hurdles of puberty, I am confident that we have laid the groundwork for a good start. I encourage you, as you seek to apply the attitudes and tips I have presented throughout this chapter, to do so prayerfully and with confidence that the Lord will give you the grace and wisdom you need to nurture your child's burgeoning sexuality.

Now, it's time to forge ahead as we examine adolescence and young adulthood.

CHAPTER SEVEN

The Vocational Years

Adolescence (Ages 15-19)

In terms of personal development, adolescence represents the period of. . . discovery of one's vocation. Both for physiological, social and cultural reasons, this period tends to be longer today than in the past. Christian parents should "educate the children for life in such a way that each one may fully perform his or her role according to the vocation received from God."

~*The Truth and Meaning of Human Sexuality*
(Quoting *Familiaris Consortio*)

As the quote above suggests, adolescence is the time of life in which we solidify our identities. During this phase, we address hard questions about the kind of people we want to become, the kind of work we would like to do, the beliefs we profess, the groups we wish to be associated with, and the kind of people with whom we wish to be most closely involved. Add how all of this relates to one's blossoming sexuality and you can begin to get a picture of why adolescence is such a tumultuous time.

For our purposes, adolescence is a kind of "puberty part two" (just when you thought it was safe to come out of the bathroom!). In puberty, we discussed the importance of giving

your young person the building blocks of identity, of giving
initial information on self-care and body awareness, and of talking about the basics of dating behavior. In adolescence, we as
parents need to continue talking about all of that, only more
so, plus we need to add a few things, including . . .

- Helping the young person find a solid sense of identity.
- Educating the teen about the real purpose of Christian
  relationships.
- Working to make your marriage be a good example of a
  Christian relationship.
- Setting appropriate boundaries around dating relation-
  ships.
- Keeping lines of communication open between parent
  and teen.
- Empowering the teen to avoid seeking substitutes for
  true intimacy.
- Helping the adolescent become fully aware of the prob-
  lems related with disordered dating or sexual relation-
  ships and how to avoid them.
- Helping the teen make good decisions about friendships
  and activities.
- Continuing to encourage the teen to develop a personal
  relationship with Christ and the Church.

Over the next few pages, we'll examine some tips that will
help you negotiate these challenges gracefully.

Helping the young person find a solid sense of identity

In the last chapter I introduced this notion in terms of helping your youth find activities she was interested in and friends
who would be supportive to her. Now I would like to develop
this idea a bit further.

Having an identity means two things:

1. That you have some idea of the values, beliefs, and characteristics you wish to be known for at the end of your life (including the kind of word that would best correspond with these values, beliefs, and characteristics).
2. Would I be able to tell, just by looking at the choices you make, the way you organize your life, and the people you associate with, what values, beliefs, and characteristics are personally important to you?

The first point determines whether or not you have at least the seeds of an identity. The second point determines the strength of that identity.

St. Francis used to tell his disciples, "Go out and preach the Gospel; use words if you must." This is the essence of the second statement above. You know that you have a strong identity if your daily life and choices actively reflect the pursuit of the values, beliefs, and characteristics that you say are important to you. Conversely, you know you have a weak identity if your life does not reflect the pursuit of those things.

Adolescence is the time in life when a young person is called to identify what he or she stands for, and what it means to live up to those standards. Likewise, it is the time in life when the adolescent learns what roles other people have, or do not have, in helping him or her pursue those ideals.

To do this, ask your young person the following questions:

1. What qualities do you want to be known for at the end of your life? (Give examples like "loving, generous, loyal, strong, courageous," etc.)
2. What decisions do you have to make on a daily basis (for example, what activities would you have to sign up for or say "no" to, what kinds of people would you need

to associate with, what groups should you choose to belong to or avoid) in order to increase the chances that you will become this person when your mature?

3. What kind of work, careers/vocations, and activities would be important opportunities to nurture those important qualities, beliefs, and values. For example: a youth who valued "courage, loyalty, and strength" would probably be interested in different activities and career paths than a youth who primarily valued, "love, generosity, gentleness, understanding."

4. What people in your life actually encourage these qualities and beliefs in you? What people in your life discourage or make you feel ashamed of those qualities or beliefs? What do you need to do about both kinds of relationships?

Obviously, this is not a discussion that you will have only once in the five-year span of time that comprises adolescence; it should be an ongoing process that unfolds with every major decision your young person faces. *Parenting with Grace* talks about how to use such a "mission statement" to gradually give your teen more and more control over his or her own choices. I would encourage you to examine the many uses of such a mission statement, as it is imperative to helping you maintain respectful discipline and good rapport with your adolescents.

Before we leave this section, I would like to say a word or two about religious vocations. Specifically, how does your teen know whether God is calling her to married life or to religious life? How does your young person know whether God is calling him to be a father, or to be Rev. Father?

This too is tied up in your young person's identity statement. Once we have clarified the values, ideals, and goals we want to exhibit in the course of our lives, we have some decisions to make. For example:

- Do the paths I want to travel down leave time for marriage and family life?

  For example: Some professions (physician, lawyer, and other intense occupations) demand a great deal of time and energy and are actually hostile to marriage and family life. (The divorce rates for such professions is astronomical.) Young people with intense passions that take up most of their time, who want to pursue careers that require a great deal of time and energy, should be strongly encouraged to evaluate the option of religious life so that they could use their gifts for the benefit of the whole Church, giving as much time and energy as they can to these pursuits, and not do so at the risk of losing or failing in their obligations to their spouses and children.

- Do I feel God calling me to have children? Or do I not have a special interest in raising my own children?

  Many teens think of the storybook ideal of marriage. That is, "I want to be married so that I can fulfill the romantic fantasy and live happily ever after." While good marriages are romantic, the main ministry of marriage is the ministry of raising children. If your youth has a special affection for children, then he or she should probably be encouraged toward marriage and family life. If, on the other hand, your child likes the romantic aspects of marriage but hasn't really given much thought to having children, he or she should be encouraged to at least investigate the possibility of religious life.

  In fact, all children should be encouraged to investigate both vocations with a prayerful attitude. We must encourage our teens to constantly seek after God's will for their lives.

- Would I do better being accountable to one person calling me on to become the person God is calling me to be, or would I like to have a community of men or women to bounce ideas off of and to give and receive encouragement from?

    If your teen would do better working intimately with one person to fulfill his/her God-given plans, dreams, and values, then he or she may be better suited for marriage. On the other hand, if your teen likes to solicit the opinions of many different people — and offer his or her opinions to many other people — on his or her path to becoming the person God created him or her to be, then your youth might be better suited for religious, community life.

Basically, these questions and others like them, are intended to help your youth understand that for the rest of his or her life he or she will be responsible for living out the values God has placed upon his or her heart. In order to do this, one needs the right kind of relationships offering just the right kind of support. Clarify the values, beliefs, and goals that your youth wishes to pursue, then help him or her discover the kind of commitment those things will require, and what kind of support will be needed to achieve those ends.

Educating the teen about the real purpose of Christian relationships

Many teens think that relationships are about finding someone to hang out with and to "make me feel good." While these things are certainly part of any romantic relationship, they are the least important part.

For the Christian, the real purpose if dating is to find the one person who is best suited to helping you become the person God created you to be — and vice versa. Once your child has created his own identity statement, ask him to evaluate his relationships in the context of it. It is a regular occurrence in my practice for parents to bring in an adolescent son or daughter and desperately ask me what they can do to separate their teen from a boyfriend or girl friend they believe to be a bad influence.

Unfortunately, there is little that they, the parents, can do directly. But by taking the time to help your teen develop an identity statement and a list of the qualities he or she would want in a partner, you can give your young person the tools he or she needs to make educated decisions for him- or herself.

One man I know had not developed an identity statement with his daughter yet. But he was in the habit of taking her to breakfast once or twice a month. During one of these breakfasts, the daughter began talking about how she was crazy about a new young man. After politely listening for a while, the father took the opportunity to ask her to come up with a list of qualities that she would want in a husband. She ticked off about four or five things, and then she started to cry.

"What's wrong?" asked the father.

Tearfully, she said, "I just realized that Mark [her boyfriend] doesn't have anything I really want in a relationship. Do you think he's bad for me?"

"Well, honey, I don't know. It's your list. I'm afraid this is going to have to be your decision. But I want you to know how proud I am of you for thinking this hard about what you want and taking relationships so seriously. That is very mature of you."

Within the week, the man's daughter broke up with her boyfriend.

As touching as this story is, you can avoid such a close call by helping your young persons come up with a wish list of the characteristics he or she would want in a mate some day. The youths can then use the first date or two to ask simple questions in the course of conversation that will help them decide whether or not this person meets their criteria.

Interestingly, my wife began using this exact method before we began dating each other. Tired of taking a hit-or-miss approach to dating, she had made a list of the qualities she wanted in a husband and a father for her future children. In our first dates, she was able to discover a lot about me because she knew what she wanted to ask. These questions helped us found our relationship around the intention of helping each other become the people we believed God wanted us to be when we grew up. This intention — developed early on in our dating relationship — became the basis for the exceptional marriage we enjoy today.

When you have taken the time to help your young persons develop an identity statement, you give them a way to check their own relationships, and you give yourself a legitimate way to inquire about the health of a relationship without seeming like a buttinsky. All you have to do is ask, "When you are with (insert name here), do you feel like he/she is helping you become more of yourself or less?" Your young persons will not resent the intrusion, because, if it's done in the right spirit, they will know that you are only helping them stay true to the values they themselves have said are important.

Working to make your marriage be a good example of a Christian relationship

You and your partner will need to continue working hard in this time to show your young people what to expect from relationships. Are you and your mate best friends? Do you work to demonstrate affection for each other throughout the day? Do you argue respectfully and effectively? Do you work well together to manage the home, the children, and your lives? Now is an especially important time to take stock of your marriage and do the work that needs to be done to make your marriage into the example it should be.

Why is this so important? Because God has given adolescents a low tolerance for hypocrisy and inconsistency. Your teens are looking for reliable models to pattern their own lives after. They will not be likely to accept your relationship advice — even sound relationship advice — if they cannot say that they would like to have a marriage that closely resembles yours.

Setting appropriate boundaries around dating relationships

Setting appropriate limits is an important part of helping your teen learn the purpose of Christian relationships. When you set limits, such as curfews or bans on certain activities, try to remember that the point of these boundaries is not merely to prevent certain sexual situations from occurring; rather, the limits are primarily in place to teach your youths how to have a Christian relationship in the first place.

On of the things that I encourage parents to do is something called the "interview." John Ream, a Catholic father and grandfather who conducts "Effective Fatherhood Seminars," recommends interviewing the people your son or daughter is dating. While it sounds ominous (As John himself jokes, "The interview begins with 'Up against the wall!' ") the interview is actually a beautiful thing that his own children — and even his nieces and the children of friends — have asked him to do for them when they reach dating age.

While Mr. Ream has most experience using the interview with the boyfriends of his daughters or other female family members, I see no reason why a husband and wife could not sit down with their son and his beloved and conduct a similar interview. I have taken the liberty of combining Mr. Ream's interview with my own reliance on an identity statement. The result looks something like this.

The mother and father make a point of meeting the young person dating their teen (for the sake of clarity, we will use this example with a daughter, but a similar format could be used with a son). This meeting should take place early in the relationship, so that you can demonstrate that you and your daughter are holding the boy up to a higher standard of behavior right from the beginning. In preparing for this encounter, the mother and father might make dinner for the younger couple or plan some other activity that would accommodate the casual yet serious nature of the meeting.

Over the course of the evening, the father should lovingly, gently, but firmly take the lead in saying to the young man dating his daughter (or, with changes, to the young woman dating his son), "I want you to know how happy I am that my daughter has found someone who helps her feel as happy as she does when she is with you. I've heard good things about you from my daughter, and I can tell that she really respects you. I wanted to meet you, because I needed to tell you something. I love this young woman [he indicates the daughter]. I would willingly give my life for her, as she is more special to me than anything I have. My wife and I have worked hard to instill values in her that will assure her of a happy and blessed life, and she herself says that every day she wants to work toward being [insert the qualities of her identity statement here]. I really respect her for that.

"I need you to understand, that when you are out with her, I am trusting you with my special treasure. Man to man, I want you to promise me that you will never take her anywhere she could be harmed, do anything intentional to harm her yourself, or be disrespectful to the values and virtues that are important to her. Will you make that promise to me?"

This is an intense and loving action that is best handled by the father. It does two things. First, it is a public proclamation of your love for your son or daughter. You are showing the suitor the exact value of the treasure he has found. This is an overwhelmingly beautiful experience for your son or daughter, who truly feels esteemed by being spoken of this way.

Second, it sends a clear message that you are not playing around. Relationships are serious business. Self-esteem, future goals, even lives can be changed forever — for better or worse — by the shortest encounter between a man and a woman. This lets the young couple know that there is more to a serious relationship than having a guaranteed date for bowling night; that a Christian relationship is ultimately about believing that you have a better chance, with your partner than without him, of becoming the person God wants you to be by the end of your life, and vice versa.

Keeping lines of communication open between parent and teen

There is a myth that says that teens need their parents less than their younger brothers and sisters. The fact is that teens need their parents more, but in different ways. Adolescents tend not to do very well with "Let's sit down and share" time, but they will share openly with a parent while they are working on projects with that parent or doing fun activities with that parent.

Make a point to work and play with your teen as much as is appropriate, while respecting at the same time his need to be with his own friends. There is nothing wrong, for example, in requiring one day per week to be "family day," in which the entire family plays or works together on things that are important to members. For the most part, these times should be reserved for family members only, although the teen may occasionally invite a friend to join in — at the parents' discretion. A great deal of sharing and bonding occurs between parents and their teens — even reluctant teens —when this kind of family time is taken. Of course, this will work better if family day has been a regular feature for your family since your teens were pubescent or younger. Even so, whenever you come to it, spending time working and recreating with your teen is the best way to make sure that the lines of communication will remain open.

Empowering the teen to avoid seeking substitutes for true intimacy

Every person seeks intimacy. Not every person finds it. Too many people mistake sex or physical affection for true intimacy. But while a satisfying sexual relationship is the fruit of an intimate marital friendship, intimacy cannot be achieved through sex alone.

Teach your children that intimacy is what happens when you work side-by-side with another person helping each other become the people that God created you to be. When you find that person of the opposite sex who is best able to help you become that person, and vice versa, you marry that person. The sexual relationship you celebrate is joyful because it is a symbol of how well you work for each other's good all day long. Under these circumstances, sex becomes a God-given language through which two people say to each other, "See how well we work together for each other's good! Even our bodies work together to celebrate our love, and make new life, and show how special we are to each other and to God."

On the other hand, when two people have sex without this commitment and intimacy, all they end up saying to each other is, "You make me feel good. You're a lot of fun to be with." Inevitably what happens is that at some point their relationship stops being fun, and so they move on to the next person. Because of this, it is important to remember that true love, true intimacy, waits for marriage to be sexual. It is only after marriage, when two people have promised to be each other's friends for life no matter what, that a sexual relationship can be healthy and good. I would encourage you to contact organizations like "True Love Waits" or purchase "Chastity rings" (rings that are worn on your teens' wedding-ring finger as a sign of their commitment to wait for true marital intimacy before engaging in sex). Don't just assume that your teen will remain a virgin until marriage because he or she is a Catholic. Celebrate their commitment to chastity with a gift like the rings I mentioned above, and a formal, prayerful promise to be faithful to the values they stand for as young Christian men and women.

I would also encourage you to give your teens good information on the psychological and physical reasons to remain virgins until marriage. For example, in an earlier chapter, I gave the case of the woman whose marriage failed because of her husband's sexual addiction. You may recall that she told her son that a good marriage takes two whole people to work, but that each time you have sex with a different person, you give a part of yourself away to that person, until pretty soon you don't have anything of yourself left, and you have nothing left to give to a spouse.

In addition to this psychological reasoning, give your teen the information he or she needs about the physiological consequences of a promiscuous life. While this includes some information on pregnancy or sexually transmitted diseases, I would suggest that there is another physiological reality that is even more significant to your teen. Allow me to explain:

In every person, there is hormone called "oxytocin." Oxtytocin has been nicknamed the "love hormone" because it is present wherever love is present. Its job is to create the loving feelings that help make bonds between two people and help them tolerate the stresses of relationships. For example, oxytocin is present when the placenta is being ejected so that the mother can bond with the baby even through the pain of childbirth. Oxytocin is present when a mother nurses her baby, which enables her to remain calm and peaceful even in the presence of a crying child. Also, oxytocin is created in male and female orgasm, and it has the effect of helping a couple keep warm feelings about each other despite the various stresses and tensions that may pull at their relationship.

The problem is this: If a couple has sex before marriage, they easily fall "under the influence" of oxytocin. In other words, they feel warmly toward each other, even when there is not cause to feel that way, and even when there are serious reasons not to. Likewise, they are not able to make reasonable judgments about whether or not this is a healthy relationship for them. I know many examples (and chances are your son or daughter knows many more examples) of young women who sleep with young men who then begin abusing them, only to find they can't leave because of the warm feelings they inexplicably have for the abuser. Or young men who have sex with a young woman who is addicted to alcohol or drugs, or cheats on them, or treats them terribly, but they can't leave these women because, inexplicably, they feel so in love with them. While there are often complex psychological factors at work here as well, one could just as easily say that the reason these two people cannot leave these destructive relationships is that they are "hopped up" on oxytocin.

In marriage, oxytocin works well because it can help two people (who have chosen well in the first place) ignore the little slights and petty irritations that accompany married life. But before marriage, oxytocin causes many couples to ignore warning signs that everyone else could see but for "some strange reason" (like being drugged by their own biochemistry) they aren't able to see for themselves until it's too late.

St. Paul tells men, "Do you not know that he who joins himself to a prostitute becomes one body with her?" (1 Cor 6:16). This is not just a spiritual truth, it is a psychological and physiological one as well. Oxytocin creates a physical bond between two people, whether they should be joined or not. Teach your children the importance of reserving this physical bond for marriage — that is, after they have already determined that the person they are with has what it takes to be a lifelong, positive, godly influence.

Helping the adolescent become fully aware of the problems related with disordered dating or sexual relationships and how to avoid them

There are many reasons that dating relationships go awry. Here are some of the more popular, along with some solutions:

1. The teen is trying to find him-/herself through dating.

Some people don't know who they are unless they are dating someone else. These people get their sense of self-worth by finding someone to love them. In their minds, they think,

"I am not very worthwhile, but I can't be all bad; after all, I'm dating!"

Encourage your teen to see how pathetic this sentiment truly is. Teach your adolescent that, as Scripture says, he is fearfully and wonderfully made. Teach your teen that God has created each one of us for a purpose and it is our job to discover and fulfill that purpose — that if we do not do this, we will be held accountable to God for having squandered our lives. Help your teen find activities that excite her, values (in the form of an identity statement) to stand and fight for, and friends to support her.

2. The teen is bored.

There is an old saying that "Idle minds are the devil's playground." As "church-lady" as this expression sounds, there is truth in it. Many times teens get into trouble because they can't think of anything else they are good at.

Besides doing all of the things I mentioned in number one above, make sure to help your teen discover his strengths and encourage his sense of competence and accomplishment. The less competent a teen feels, the more "bored" he will complain of being. Teach competence, and avoid the disordered relationships that result from the attempt to ease the pain of boredom.

3. The teen is trying to prove his/her masculinity/ femininity or maturity.

Many teens get in over their heads sexually because they are trying to prove something to themselves or their friends. "I am man enough to get a woman." " I am woman enough to seduce a man." "I am mature enough to have a baby."

Young people who have such ideas were often given a very poor education regarding what it really means to be a man or woman. Re-read the chapter on middle childhood to make sure you are covering your bases on this subject. And teach your teen that to be a real man or a real woman means standing up for his or her values, and working for the good of the people around him or her.

4. It just happened.

Many times teens will tell me that "I didn't mean to have sex; it just happened." Really, what they are saying is, "I really wanted to do it, but I can't admit that I really wanted to do it, so I'll just pretend that I accidentally fell into it." Let your teen know well in advance that you won't buy this story.

Teach your adolescent that there is no such thing as "it just happened." Before a person gets burned by a fire, there are a million chances to pull back from the fire. Before a person slams his car into another car, there were a million chances to have driven more responsibly. The person who makes responsible choices will not find himself in compromising positions. Teach your child what "the near occasion of sin" means. For example, in his work, *Intimate Behavior: A Zoologist's Classic Study of Human Behavior*, Desmond Morris has 12 stages in a healthy physical relationship (N.B. these stages are also covered in David Joy's book *Becoming a Man*); each stage corresponds to a level of intimacy, and each level must be attended to before the next level can be reached with any success (so no skipping steps or hurrying through them). Stages 1-5 are also appropriate levels of friendship, but no unmarried persons can safely go beyond stage 9 before they have gotten too close — that is, they are engaging in a near occasion of sin. Let's take a look at the stages that will help your teen know how far is too far and at what stage of the relationship.

The Twelve Stages of Physical Intimacy

(1) Eye to Body

This is not the lascivious stare of a predator, but the innocent first look when you notice that space is being filled up by a person. There is no sexual content to this sighting.

(2) Eye to Eye

Eye contact is crucial to gauge someone's interest. Remember that game where you catch someone's eye, then look away, then do it over again?

(3) Voice to Voice

This is, perhaps, the hardest stage: to strike up a conversation and learn about someone is a prerequisite for *real* intimacy. Tell your teen that he or she should stay at this level for 4 to 6 months because to go further before having successfully completed this stage is to put sexual feelings before true intimacy (i.e., the friendship that comes from knowing that someone is willing to help you become the person God created you to be — and vice versa). This is the stage in which you learn about someone without your judgment being clouded by all those warm fuzzy love chemicals that are released in skin-to-skin contact. This is where you make judgment calls as to whether or not you like this person's character, habits, attitudes, etc. Failure to take this step seriously leads to disaster.

(4) Hand to Hand

Now the young man and young woman are a couple and "joined" in a public way; if they break up now, people will ask "where is so-and-so?" This is also where those love chemicals start pouring in. This is also a stage of friendship; for example, young girls in Europe are often seen walking hand-in-hand with their best friends.

(5) Arm to Shoulder.

This is the "arms around each other" look, also seen in a football huddle. Guys are comfortable doing this step with their buddies. Between a woman and a man it is the physical, public way to say, "We are joined in a special kind of friendship." It joins a couple closer in the public eye.

Now we approach those stages that leave behind mere platonic friendship and begin to express a more romantic kind of intimacy.

(6) Arm to Waist

The elbows are crossed behind the back, hands fall to waist, the couple is "x-linked" together. Conversation is more intimate and serious. Commit now or break up. At this point, if the relationship is broken off, there will be anger and grieving and depression.

(7) Face to Face (mouth to mouth)

(IT IS VERY IMPORTANT TO BE SURE ALL THE STAGES PRIOR TO THIS HAVE BEEN DEVELOPED!) Intimate kissing serves a "cementing purpose." Kissing triggers sexual arousal, and once arousal is experienced, stages 1-6 are abandoned and critical work that may need to be completed in the relationship is left by the wayside. If this stage is rushed into, premature sexual relationships usually occur. The basic friendship will be shallow and the foundation weak. Kissing is special; don't give it away.

(8) Hand to Head

This is actually more intimate than hand to hand. Think of a mother caressing a child's face. The gentle stroking of a lover's face is a very intimate and tender action. In Asian countries, it is disrespectful for anyone other than a family member to touch a child's head because of the intimacy level.

(9) Hand to Body

By now, you are comfortable with each other; a bear hug, a shoulder massage, a stroke on the arm are all acceptable forms of this hand-to-body stage. This does not include any kind of "petting" or genital touching, which is reserved for the next few stages.

Let your teen know that if he or she goes any further than this, he or she is entering into the stages of sexual arousal (stages 10-12 directly relate to foreplay and intercourse: stage 10 involves touching and kissing the breasts, stage 11 is genital touching, and stage 12 is intercourse). It is unacceptable for unmarried couples to go past stage nine without crossing "the point of no return" that will most likely lead to sex. Likewise, unless a person builds the friendship required by the first nine stages, sex is nothing but eroticism: using and being used by another person.

If your teen is serious about maintaining his or her values and becoming the person God wants him or her to be, teach him or her not to go past stage nine before marriage, or, for that matter, not to date anyone who thinks too casually of going beyond stage nine before marriage. Teach them to avoid these situations, not because they are bad, but because unless they are enjoyed at the right time in the right way (in the context of a friendship so strong that one has to take vows before God to live it out), these joys can be spoiled, just like the Golden Narnian Apple I spoke of in an earlier chapter. And that would be a tragedy.

Helping the teen make good decisions about friendships and activities

In the last chapter, we talked about the importance of connecting your children with various activities that were important to them, and giving them the tools to discern which friendships were beneficial, and which were not.

Continue to remind your child how to discern his or her interests and his or her own friendships. As much as possible, resist the temptation to heavy-handedly insist that your child not associate with certain peers (this often makes those peers only that much more attractive). Rather, continue to build rapport with your teen by inviting him or her to work and recreate alongside of you as much as possible, and in those times, help your son or daughter decide for him- or herself whether certain friendship or activities are helping them stay faithful to their own mission statement or not.

Continuing to encourage the teen to develop a personal relationship with Christ and the Church

Finally and most importantly, continue to foster both an emotional and intellectual faith in your son and daughter. Your teens will have a million questions about God and the faith. Teach them how to answer those questions. Books like Matt Pinto's *Did Adam Have a Belly Button?* or MaryBeth Bonnaci's *Real Love* or *We're on A Mission From God*, or Keith and Tammy Keiser's *Sex: The Incredible Gift* or other books on beginning apologetics or Catholic relationships are helpful because they are written to address the most common questions that young people have about the faith and what that faith means to their life and relationships.

Likewise, continue to encourage and support your youth's membership in Catholic youth groups like Antioch, Life Teen, or other groups. Such gatherings of faithful young people provide your son or daughter with needed peer support to keep their faith vital even when they stop riding on your coattails.

Wrapping It Up

In the preceding pages and chapters, I have tried to address some of the most important issues facing parents as we struggle to raise sexually whole and holy kids. While no book could cover all the information you need, here is my hope: that, by looking at sexuality as a construct of many different characteristics evolving over the course of your child's life in many different arenas in addition to the genital ones, I have broadened your understanding of what it takes to raise a child to conduct his sexual self — at all stages — with love and responsibility.

In the next chapter, I will address some common problems that can emerge with sexuality and offer some tips to help you as you confront these problems.

CHAPTER EIGHT

Some Common Questions and Concerns

In my work as director of the Pastoral Solutions Institute, I regularly field questions from parents who have concerns about all aspects of marriage and family life, including questions about sexuality, either their own or their children's. Whenever possible, I have covered certain topics, like masturbation and pre-marital sex, in the body of this book. In the following pages, I would like to turn to some questions that I did not have the opportunity to address as thoroughly as I would have liked in the previous chapters. For example:

- Why is artificial birth control wrong?
- Why is homosexuality wrong, and what should I do if my child experiences same-sex attraction?
- How can I talk to my child about abortion?
- I found my child looking at pornography. What should I do?
- What are some signs of sexual abuse? What should I do if I think my child has been abused?
- How do I know when to seek professional help for problems with my child or in my marriage?

- and many other serious questions like these.

Let's take these questions one at a time.

Why is artificial birth control wrong?

First, let's define our terms. Artificial birth control includes all chemical or mechanical methods (the pill, condoms, IUDs, cervical caps, sponges, spermicidal creams, etc.) that actively seek to destroy any chance that a couple will have a baby when they make love.

The simplest explanation I have found for why these things are wrong is this. Several years ago, there was a popular song called *Tell Me, Have You Ever Really (Really, Really) Ever Loved a Woman?* I believe it was the theme to the movie *The Scent of a Woman*. In it, there is a line that says,

> *"When you can see your unborn children in her eyes then you really love a woman."*

The Church agrees. There is no love more beautiful than the love that says, "I see my children in your eyes." A love that says, to paraphrase Scott Hahn, "I want to celebrate a love with you that is so powerful that in nine months it has to be given its own name."

Artificial birth control, on the other hand, sends a very different message. It says, "I want to make you feel wonderful, and I want you to make me feel wonderful, *but keep your rotten kids to yourself.*" This is a tragic message to send a lover. "I don't see my children in your eyes. I don't want all of you. Can't we just be happy with the parts that make us feel good right now?"

The Church says we deserve better. The Church teaches us that we should always celebrate the kind of intense, passionate, God-given love that is so powerfully profound that it allows us to see our children in our lover's eyes for as long as this is possible. We deserve to know that the person we are giving ourselves to wants all of us, especially the children God has placed in our hearts.

So, why is Natural Family Planning okay? Isn't that just Catholic birth control?

No, it is most definitely not Catholic birth control. With artificial birth control, there is no prayer, there is no discernment, there is no discussion, there is only, "We have decided not to have children, indefinitely."

While it is true that Natural Family Planning is over 99% effective as a method of postponing pregnancy, the attitude of a couple properly practicing NFP is quite different from the attitude of a contracepting couple. With NFP, the couple is always able see their children in the eyes of their lover, but they are taught how to balance this profound desire with the need to provide a firm foundation of love from which those children could be born.

As far as the Church is concerned, there are two purposes of marriage: (1) building a union between a man and woman that is so strong and beautiful that it mirrors the loving relationship between Christ and his Church, and (2) working with God to bring new life into the world. Both "ends of marriage" (unitive and procreative, as they are called) are of equal dignity in the eyes of the Church, and the couple must see to it that they are constantly strengthening both, because both are essential for creating the "community of love" the Church calls families to be. In other words, as far as the community of love goes, without children, there is no community, but without a strong unity between the couple, there is no love. Either way, the "community of love" is hobbled. Because of this, NFP couples are encouraged to ask God the following question *every month*: "Lord, are you asking us to bring another life into the community of love we have? Or are you calling us, this month, to strengthen this community in some way, so that any future children would find a warm, loving home to be born into?"

Every day of every month, the NFP couple is encouraged to be mindful of and foster their communication, romance, generosity, friendship, and prayer life — so that they can first celebrate the kind of enviable, joyful, grace-filled marriage that would then be a hospitable and welcoming environment for the children the lovers still see in each other's eyes. Metaphorically speaking, on the one hand NFP stops a couple from becoming the kind of husband and wife who keep a perfect-looking house but never invite any company to warm their home; and on the other hand it stops a couple from being the kind of husband and wife who invite company to a home that is trashed, uncomfortable, and hostile to the eyes, ears, nose, and most importantly, the heart.

No pun intended, but artificial birth control breeds the kind of people who have a hundred teddy bears on the wall and a thousand decorative toys on the mantle but forbid children to play with any of them. In other words, it breeds infantile, selfish, materialistic, pseudo-grown-ups who look good on the outside but have no depth, no soul. Furthermore, it causes a couple to be cavalier about their relationship, believing that there is no problem that can't be glossed over by sexing one's way through it. As long as the oxytocin mill is producing enough of the couple's drug of choice, who cares if they don't communicate, don't pray, don't plan their future together, don't work well together to run the home and raise the children — who cares if they aren't real friends?

By contrast, rather than merely being about having or not having children, NFP, if practiced properly, empowers a couple constantly to be mindful of the "community of love" that the Church calls them to celebrate in their home, and enables them to always see their children — those already born and those yet to be —in their lover's eyes.

This is just the tip of the iceberg, of course. But are you at least beginning to understand the differences between NFP and artificial birth control?

What about masturbation? Why is it such a big deal?

The Church tells us that masturbation is a serious problem (see *Catechism of the Catholic Church*, #2352). But let's face it. Saying that masturbation is a "serious problem" raises hoots of indignation, irritation, and worse from a world that celebrates books like, *Sex for One* — a popular text on the "joys" of masturbation. How could something done for one's own pleasure in the privacy of one's own room be problematic — much less, seriously so? Is it simply that the Church is a big killjoy with nothing better to do than to assail the privacy of innocent people? Of course not. So? What's the problem?

Most people begin masturbating in adolescence — and granted, at first occurrence it is often the result of a basically healthy curiosity about one's changing body and the new sensations one is experiencing. In this form, masturbation, while certainly a distortion of what God created our sexuality to be, is questionably sinful (it lacks the requirement of full knowledge) and most likely not something to send yourself — or your child — to the psychiatric hospital for (see *Catechism of the Catholic Church*, #2352 paragraph, 2, and *The Encyclopedia of Catholic Doctrine*, p. 432). Even so, it is not completely without danger. Since masturbation is often the first sexual experience a person has, it can establish some very negative sexual precedents that become stronger as the frequency of masturbation increases: among them, that sex has no purpose beyond pleasuring oneself; that —since one often masturbates to pictures or images — people are basically things to be used to pleasure oneself; that sex is a powerful drug that can be used for venting a variety of negative emotions; that masturbating is easier than pursuing real intimacy. Any one of these lessons can set the stage for compulsive masturbation, which is a serious problem and, quite possibly, serious sin (*Catechism*, #2352). So, what's a parent to do? Besides reviewing the previous sections in this book that have already dealt with this topic (please refer to the subject index in *Beyond the Birds and the Bees*), the following tips will help you assist your children as they struggle to understand their sexuality.

1. Take a Breath.

    The first thing you need to do is remain calm. As I have already pointed out, the earliest episodes of masturbation usually occur as a result of ignorance and curiosity. Shrieking about "perversion" will not make the problem go away; in fact, it will probably make it worse. The only difference will be that you won't know about it. Approach your child with the warmth and affection of a teacher whose student just added 2+2 and — try as he might — only got 3.14159.

2. Teach Your Child the Spiritual Context of His Feelings.

    After you have asked God's help to be a compassionate teacher to His child, remember that the Holy Father, Pope John Paul II, told us that God reveals Himself to us through our bodies (see Pope John Paul's

"Theology of the Body"). Teach your children the true meaning of the sensations they are experiencing. Let them know that at this stage of their lives, sexual feelings are God's way of saying, "Start getting ready. I have someone in mind for you to love and be loved by. I want you to spend the next few years learning how to be a good help-mate to the one I have chosen for you."

Explain to your children that they can waste the time God has given them to prepare by pursuing their own selfish "pleasures," or they can respond to God's call by learning more about healthy relationships, reading age-appropriate literature on Christian marriage and sexuality, and learning to be a better friend to the young men and women God places in their path.

Help your children to understand that when they experience arousal, they are feeling the voice of God speaking through their bodies. He is asking them to pray, both for their soul-mates and for themselves, that one day they may find true happiness with each other and God.

Acknowledge that the struggle to overcome selfish desires is a difficult one, but that if God is giving them these feelings, He is confident that they are capable of learning to use them responsibly. And of course, before, during, and after this discussion, keep praying that your child will grow in age, wisdom, and grace.

3. Encourage the Three Strengths.

Children who develop problems with compulsive/habitual masturbation tend to exhibit weaknesses in three areas: they lack mature, effective ways to express emotion; they tend to be socially inept; and they tend to be sheltered even from positive, Christian sexual education. You can't keep constant tabs on your children's genitals — God forbid — but you *can* encourage their healthy sexual education, socialization, and emotional facility. In fact, the Church obligates you to do this (see *The Truth and Meaning of Human Sexuality*, and *Familiaris Consortio*). Sign your kids (girls *and* boys) up for an NFP class; buy them books on Christian relationships; encourage their memberships in clubs, teams, and other outlets where they can learn more about friendship and responsibility. Teach them how to express their emotions freely and respectfully. If you yourself have difficulty modeling these strengths, do some reading, some praying, or maybe even get some counseling. Teachers need to stay at least one chapter ahead of their students or they will be dismissed as irrelevant. In fact, the wise parents will be working to develop these strengths in their child *years* before they see little Johnny wander into the bathroom with a copy of *Cosmo*. An once of prevention is worth a pound of cure.

As I have asserted throughout the book, chastity is a skill to be taught and practiced, just like reading and math. While teaching your child this skill, keep your wits about you, your sense of humor handy, and God at your side. With the Lord's help, we can all be the skilled, compassionate teachers we need to be to help our children become the "Masters of Their Domains."

What if I catch my son or daughter with pornography?

Pornography is everywhere, and with the internet it is often a keystroke away for a curious young mind. As with dealing with masturbation, the most important thing to do when dealing with the issue of pornography is to remain calm.

First, you should admit to your son or daughter (N.B.: though boys are still more regular viewers of pornography, there is evidence to support a growing interest in pornography among teenage girls as well) that the bodies they are looking at are beautiful. God has blessed the people in those photographs with His beauty, and that is a good thing. Tell your young person that you are not objecting to the beauty of their bodies; rather, you are objecting to the way they are using their bodies.

There are many examples of nude paintings depicting biblical scenes and other themes that have been done by many great artists. Nude paintings and sculptures can even be found in the Vatican. These displays are not pornographic or even immodest, because the intention is to give glory to God and the beauty of His creation. By contrast, pornography's only intention is to make us look at another person as an object for our satisfaction. This is what makes the nudity of pornography sinful. It teaches us to see others as things to be used and disposed of when we are done with them. It teaches selfishness.

The best way I know to "spoil" pornography for youngsters is to teach them to see the person behind the images, to expose the sadness and pathology that lies beneath the glossy, air-brushed photographs. Gently and seriously, ask your youth, "Would you ever want someone to take a picture of you like that?" Assuming that they say "No," go on to ask your child why. Chances are, your child will say something like, "That would be gross" or, "I would be embarrassed."

Tell your child that he or she is absolutely right. God gave us that sense of modesty to keep us from using our bodies in wrong ways — in ways that would allow us to be used or mistreated by others. Now, ask your child why somebody else would ignore that natural feeling of modesty and pose for pictures like that? Chances are, your son or daughter will not know why, or perhaps he or she thinks that those models simply enjoy posing that way.

Explain that there are many reasons that people pose for pictures, but none of them are good. Many of the people in those pictures were victims of sexual abuse. At some point in their lives, they were forced to have sex with a family member, a friend, or a stranger, and the pain of that experience has taught them to ignore the feelings of modesty that God has given them. Some of the people in those pictures believe that the only way they can be loved is if they pose in that way and let others do disgusting things to them. Others either love or need money so desperately that they would do anything to get it, including show themselves in a shocking way, or allow other people to pose them that way just to get money. Still others have learned to hate men or women and use their bodies as a way of getting power over them.

Tell your child that when we look at pornography — or worse, masturbate to it — as far as the persons in the pictures are concerned, we become their abuser, their victimizer, or the person who pays them money to act that way. Every time we look at pornography, not only do we inadvertently encourage those models and others like them to continue to allow themselves to be hurt that way, but we become more selfish, and we start to think of other people, people we should be loving and working to help, as *things* to give us pleasure.

Encourage your child to go to confession to confess the sin of lust, which is looking at another person as an object. Encourage your child to offer a prayer for the person he or she saw in the picture, that God would give them His love, so that they would no longer feel like they had to do those things to get people's attention. Remind your child that God's purpose of sexual attraction is to remind us to use our bodies to work for the good of others. And as a consequence, ask your child to come up with, and practice, several ways that he or she could work for the good of his or her opposite-sex peers or siblings (e.g., speak respectfully or offer some specific, simple acts of service).

What should I tell my teen about sexually transmitted diseases?

Many parents tell their children about sexually transmitted diseases (STDs) as a way of trying to frighten them into living a "chaste life." This is chastity as repression, and it should be avoided. Besides, it doesn't work. Teens think they are indestructible. They will never get an STD. That only happens to other people.

When you talk about STDs, teach your youth that STDs are what happens when people use sex in the wrong way. When people make foolish choices, like having sex with people before marriage, bad things can happen. God does not cause these things to happen as punishment; in fact, He tries to warn us about them, to prevent them from happening to us in the first place. But if people choose to follow their own counsel instead of God's, then bad things happen, including STDs.

It is a bit like a parent telling a child not to run into the street. The parent tells the child this so that he will not get hurt, but if the child runs into the street anyway, chances are he will get hit by a car. The parent didn't send the car to punish the child. That's just what happens when you do not give a busy street the respect it deserves. In the same way, God tells us to save ourselves for marriage for many reasons. One of those reasons is that having sex with people — especially lots of people (but it can only take one sometimes) — before marriage can make us sick. Some of those sicknesses cause lifelong pain and shame.

Some of those sicknesses prevent a woman from ever having a baby. Some of those sickness cause death. All of those sicknesses make people very miserable and make God very sad.

Just as the only way to keep ourselves from getting hit by a car is not to run into the street (and not simply to wear a big plastic bubble that supposedly prevents us from getting hurt when we get hit); the only way to guarantee that we will not get hit with an STD is to save ourselves for marriage, and to look for a partner who has saved him- or herself for marriage as well.

What should I tell my child about abortion?

To deal with this issue, I would like to relate a personal experience.

I was driving through Pittsburgh with my family when we passed Magee Women's Hospital. Outside there was a large number of abortion protesters, and my then six-year-old son piped up from the back seat, "Why are all those people standing around with those baby signs?"

According to developmental psychologists, children as young as four and five begin demonstrating a basic understanding of mortality and can even be fairly comfortable discussing serious questions of life and death. Still, this was not a question I wanted to answer. First, I tried an honest evasion. "Well," I said, "all those people love babies very much, and they want to tell the world about it."

Such honest evasions are perfectly acceptable ways to answer questions from young children, who sometimes trip over things we aren't sure they are ready to handle. Unfortunately, though he would have a year ago, my son wasn't buying it. "But, Dad," he said, "*we* love babies, but we don't walk around with big signs about it!"

Sigh. The good news is that my wife and I had laid the groundwork for answering this question over the last few years by teaching our children how precious life is. Young children are always fascinated with infants, often pointing out, "Look at the little baby!" Lisa and I have always tried to turn these times into simple, teachable moments by saying what a gift babies are, and by making a fuss about how good God is for giving people the gift of life. It looked as if that foundation was going to be put to the test.

My wife and I explained that the "sign people," as he had taken to calling them, were there because they loved children and wanted the hospital to stop doing something to babies called abortion. Then we stopped. We wanted to let him take the lead in telling us how much he wanted to know. We wouldn't hold the truth back, but we weren't about to give him more than he was ready for (or, for that matter, we were ready for). At first he was confused. He thought we were talking about adoption. But when we explained that abortion was very different, and unlike adoption, a "very bad and sad thing," he asked what abortion was.

We started by reminding him of the times we told him that babies were a very special gift from God. Then we explained that some people didn't know this. They were afraid of having babies, and so they would go to certain doctors and ask them to stop their baby from being born. He asked how, and we explained that the doctor would do an abortion, "an operation that kills a baby while he is still in his mommy's tummy." He was appalled. The questions came pouring out: "Why would they do that? Why don't they just give the baby to somebody who wants one? They could give him to me!" And so on. We answered each question as simply and honestly as we could, letting him take the lead.

Next came the fantasy solutions one can expect from young children when they are confronted with injustice. "I'm going to go up to those mommies and doctors and tell them to stop and if they don't, I'll punch them in the nose!" We told him that we understood how he felt — that we sometimes felt the same way — but we explained that most of the mommies who have abortions are either afraid, don't know any better, or feel alone and unloved and don't think anyone will help them. We asked him, considering this, what he thought God would want us to do for those mommies. "Love them and help them?" he tentatively asked. "That's right. That was a very thoughtful answer," we said.

For the next five minutes we talked about some simple ways we could help. We could pray. We could join the "sign people" sometimes, like mommy and daddy did before he was born. And then my wife remembered that the local pro-life center was asking for help sorting and folding donated infant and maternity clothing. Our son and daughter are becoming expert laundry folders, so she asked him if he would want to go and help the center get clothes ready for the moms and their babies. He was enthusiastic. We promised him that we would follow this up in the coming week, and then we prayed. He asked to lead. "Dear Jesus, Please help those mommies know You love them and help them love their babies too. Hail Mary . . ."

Sitting in the back seat, our three-year-old daughter was privy to this conversation, and uncharacteristically quiet throughout. We were wondering what she made of it all when, after the prayer, she finally spoke. "Those signs had cute babies!"

"Yes, Honey. They did. Isn't God wonderful for making babies so special?"

While the above deals with talking to younger children about abortion, I hope that it will provide you with some helpful hints for addressing this painful topic with your kids. Beyond this, though, I would like to address one more matter, and that is how to overcome the ridiculous pro-abortion slogan "My body, my choice."

In an earlier chapter, I described the "hug talk" as a way of explaining sex. In that talk, I referred to the uterus as a special room inside the woman's body which God created to be the babies' first room. God created that "room" for children (that is its primary function after all) and God asks the woman to take care of that "room" for any children He chooses to give her. That part of her body does not belong to her. It is God's gift to the children He wants to give her. She is merely the custodian.

Tell your child to think of it this way. Imagine that he inherited a large sum of money from a rich, distant relative. But, because he was too young too handle all that money, it was placed in a trust in your name until he was old enough to claim it for himself. Now, imagine that while the money was in your name, you spent it all. Would that be right? Why not? After all, the money was in your name, wasn't it?

Of course, the answer to this question is that even though the money was in your name, it was not your money. It belonged to the child, and you were obliged to keep it well for him. The same is true of the uterus (or of breastmilk, for that matter). God gives a woman certain things that will allow her to care for His children. She does not own those things; she is simply holding them in trust until God sends a child to claim them. When the child shows up, justice requires that we give what is rightfully the child's to the child. Not to do so is a terrible offense to the child — and to God.

Anyway, as Scripture says, "None of us lives to himself" (Rom 14:7). We all belong to God, and not to ourselves, and just because something is in our bodies doesn't mean it belongs to us. This is especially true of those parts (and products) of a woman's body which God created to be held "in trust" for the child.

Why is homosexuality wrong, and what can I do if my child experiences same-sex attraction?

This is an extremely sensitive and complicated question, and I do not have the time or space to do anything but deal with it in the most cursory way and point you to some exceptional resources to help guide you in dealing with this issue.

In order for sex to be healthy and holy, it must be both unitive and procreative. Homosexual acts are neither; therefore, they are sinful. They are inherently selfish uses of God's gift of sexuality.

While there are many theories regarding the origin of homosexuality in a person, no one knows for certain the one cause, or if there even is one. Regardless of this, the Church encourages all unmarried people, including those who struggle with same-sex attraction, to abstain from sex. While some people who have struggled with same-sex attraction have overcome this struggle and gone on to live successfully as heterosexual men and women who marry and have children, the Church does not require persons with same-sex attraction to do this unless they feel God calling them to do so. The Church merely holds all persons to the same level of chastity, regardless of sexual orientation.

If your child has questions about same-sex attraction, or feels that he or she might be struggling with such feelings, I would advise you to turn to resources such as the book *Beyond Gay* by David Morrison, or to groups like *Courage* (a faithful Catholic organization, founded by Father John Harvey, that helps people with same-sex attraction to lead a chaste life), and *Encourage* (Courage's sister organization for parents with children who exhibit same-sex attraction). Courage and Encourage both have internet chat groups as well as local chapters in dioceses across the country.

The only thing I would like to add is to say that many Christians seem to reserve a special kind of hatred for homosexuality. This is wrong, and it is condemned by the Church. While acting on same-sex attraction is an objectively grave moral disorder, the *Catechism of the Catholic Church* teaches us that people with same-sex attraction, ". . . must be accepted with respect, compassion, and sensitivity."

While it is true that the homosexual person is responsible before God when he or she acts on these disordered urges, it is also true that we will be held accountable to God for every act of cruelty, joke, or uncharitable attitude we display toward anyone, including our brothers and sisters in Christ, who struggles with same-sex attraction. None of us is free from sin. None of us is free to cast stones at anyone else. If your child is struggling with same-sex attraction, contact the resources listed above to get the support you need to offer faithful, compassionate, sensitive responses to your child's concerns.

What should I know about sexual abuse?

Sexual abuse is a very real and very painful problem. It can be difficult to discover, owing to the shame that victims experience and their tendency to keep things quiet, either for fear that they will get in trouble or for fear that the abuser will cause them even more harm.

The perpetrator of sexual abuse is sometimes a stranger,

but is most often a trusted friend or relative of the child and has often been the victim of abuse him- or herself.

Although it is wise to proceed cautiously with accusations of abuse, you must always take seriously any claims your child makes about having been abused or touched inappropriately. However, since it is rare for a child to come forward freely with a report of sexual abuse, you should also be aware of the signs that could indicate possible abuse. Please take care, though. Just because your child exhibits any of the following signs does not mean that he or she has been sexually abused. It simply means that you should investigate the possibility further with a professional, like a physician and/or qualified therapist.

Children who have been sexually abused — or whose sexual boundaries have been offended in some other, serious way — often display sexual knowledge far beyond their years. They often seem obsessed with sexual play or conduct themselves in a grossly flirtatious or sexual manner that is inappropriate to their age and stage. In addition to this, many children who have been abused become obsessed with masturbation, or engage in exhibitionism (for example, regularly exposing themselves to neighborhood children or teachers). Likewise, some children who have been abused develop an obsessive tendency to rub their genitals against furniture or the family pet — even if fully clothed.

While there are other signs, these are the most serious. If you see several of them present in your child, or if your child tells you that he or she had been touched or dealt with inappropriately, you should immediately contact your family doctor to arrange for a physical examination of your child. Following that evaluation, you may also consider consulting a local therapist who is expert in the field of child sexual abuse if symptoms persist.

How do I know when I need to seek professional help?

The Vatican document *The Truth and Meaning of Human Sexuality* recommends that parents be willing to seek the advice of qualified professionals, including pastors, educators, counselors, and physicians, whenever necessary, as long as these sources are faithful to the teachings of the Church and do not seek to usurp the primary and "inalienable" right of the parents to oversee their children's education in love.

While it should be obvious that professional help would be indicated for any of the more serious sexual problems, such as same-sex attraction, cross-dressing, gender-identity issues, obsessive masturbation, exhibitionism, sexual abuse, incest, and the like, I would recommend that parents also seek outside counsel whenever they feel frustrated by a more common problem of sexual development. Because the sexual education of your children is so important and touches on so many areas of your children's lives, you will want to make sure to do it properly. While it will be your duty to prayerfully weigh any advice you are given, do not hesitate to seek outside advice whenever any problem arises that you are not completely confident you are handling as well as you could.

In addition to local resources which your diocesan family life or Catholic Charities office can put you in touch with, the Couple to Couple League is a good and faithful source of information for parents. They even offer their own chastity curriculum. You may contact them for more information on these and other programs by calling (513) 661-2000. Likewise, if you would like to discuss concerns about your or your children's sexuality with a counselor, please feel free to contact me at the Pastoral Solutions Institute, ph. (740) 266-6461.

Epilogue

Thoughts for the Continuing Journey

It has been my hope throughout *Beyond the Birds and the Bees* to give you some practical assistance and perspective on what it takes to raise children who are capable of celebrating a joyful, loving, responsible, healthy, and holy sexuality. By no means do I foster any illusions that I have given you all there is to know on the subject, nor do I presume to be offering the final word on the matter.

Fostering a healthy and holy sexuality in your children is an ongoing journey that begins with doing what is necessary to get your own sexual life in order. It continues with passing those healthy attitudes on to your children, giving honest, faithful information about the physical, emotional, relational, and spiritual aspects, as well as making every effort to encourage all of the qualities that foster strong character. Further, for this training to "take" it must be done in a home where affection and affirmation is in abundant supply as well as "a respect for others, a sense of justice, cordial openness, dialogue, generous service, solidarity, and all the other values which help people live life as a gift" ("Gospel of Life").

As you continue your journey, it is my wish that the Lord will grant you His wisdom and grace, first to enjoy a solid, loving marital relationship, and second, to be able to pass your hard-won lessons of love and responsibility on to your children. If *Beyond the Birds and the Bees* has given you validation for the excellent job you are already doing, some new points to consider, or some new techniques to apply, then I am both gratified and grateful to you for inviting me to walk alongside you for this part of your journey. It is my prayer and hope that the Lord will, as St Paul says, continue to supply all your needs according to His riches in Christ Jesus (cf. Phil 4:19), so that you will be empowered to raise children of good character, strong spirits, and a healthy, holy sexuality.

A Word From the Author

Dear Friends,

I hope you enjoyed this book, but everyone needs a little help from time to time. If you are struggling to apply your faith to tough, family, or personal problems, *The Pastoral Solutions Institute* can help.

Through the Institute, I work with an advisory board of solidly Catholic psychotherapists, theologians, and physicians who specialize in finding Catholic answers to life's difficult questions.

Our effective telephone counseling program, informative resources, and dynamic seminars incorporate cutting-edge psychology and orthodox Catholic theology to help you find peace in your life. The Institute has helped hundreds of people just like you who are coping with marriage and family problems, depression, anxiety, sexual issues, problem habits, grief and loss, parenting questions, and ethical dilemmas.

Call today for more information on counseling, seminars, books and tapes, and other resources. Let us help you brighten your world with the healing light of Christ.

Yours in Christ,

Gregory K. Popcak, MSW, LCSW

Director, Pastoral Solutions Institute

Telephone (740) 266-6461

Website: www.exceptionalmarriages.com

Resources

For Better . . . Forever! A Catholic Guide to Lifelong Marriage. Gregory K. Popcak and Lisa Popcak (Huntington, IN: Our Sunday Visitor, 1999)

Parenting with Grace: The Catholic Parent's Guide to Raising (almost) Perfect Kids. Gregory K. Popcak (Huntington, IN: OSV, 2000)

The Exceptional Seven Percent: Nine Secrets of the World's Happiest Couples. Gregory K. Popcak (New York: Kensington/Citadel, 2000)

Good News About Sex and Marriage. Christopher West (Ann Arbor, MI: Servant, 1990)

Real Love. Mary Beth Bonacci (San Francisco: Ignatius, 1996)

We're On A Mission From God. Mary Beth Bonacci (San Francisco: Ignatius, 1996)

Sex: The Incredible Gift. Keith and Tammy Kiser (Huntington, IN: OSV, 1996)

Catholic Sexual Ethics. Lawler, May, et al. (Huntington, IN: OSV, 1985)

The Catholic Vision of Love (4 vols.). Rev. Kris D. Stubna (Huntington, IN: OSV, 1996)

Know Your Body. Charles Norris, M.D. (Huntington, IN: OSV, 1983)

Talking to Youth About Sexuality. Mike Aquilina (Huntington, IN: OSV, 1995)

The Truth and Meaning of Human Sexuality. (Vatican Pontifical Council on the Family, 1999)

The Couple to Couple League
For information on Natural Family Planning and chastity education. Ph. (513) 471-2000

Index

Notes

Notes

Notes

Notes

Notes

Notes

The perfect marriage isn't just a myth. You can have a
loving, fulfilling, life-long relationship. Learn how with
this practical guide to Catholic marriage.
0-87973-688-7 (688), paper, 256 pp.

To order from Our Sunday Visitor:
Toll free: 1-800-348-2440
E-mail: osvbooks@osv.com
Website: www.osv.com

Availability of books subject to change without notice.

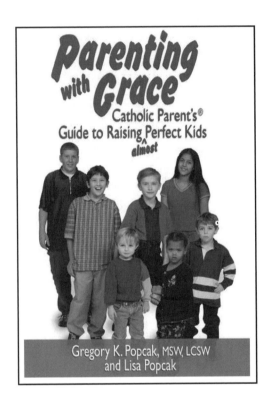

Discover your own God-given instruction manual for
creating a highly individualized, completely Catholic
parenting plan for your children.
0-87973-730-1 (730), paper, 336 pp.

To order from Our Sunday Visitor:
Toll free: 1-800-348-2440
E-mail: osvbooks@osv.com
Website: www.osv.com

Availability of books subject to change without notice.

Our Sunday Visitor...

Your Source for Discovering
the Riches of the Catholic Faith

Our Sunday Visitor has an extensive line of materials for young children, teens, and adults. Our books, Bibles, booklets, CD-ROMs, audios, and videos are available in bookstores worldwide.

To receive a FREE full-line catalog or for more information, call **Our Sunday Visitor** at **1-800-348-2440**. Or write, **Our Sunday Visitor /** 200 Noll Plaza / Huntington, IN 46750.

- -

Please send me: ___A catalog

Please send me materials on:

___Apologetics and catechetics   ___Reference works

___Prayer books   ___Heritage and the saints

___The family   ___The parish

Name_____

Address_____Apt._____

City_____State_____Zip_____

Telephone (   ) _____

A19BBABP

- -

Please send a friend: ___A catalog

Please send a friend materials on:

___Apologetics and catechetics   ___Reference works

___Prayer books   ___Heritage and the saints

___The family   ___The parish

Name_____

Address_____Apt._____

City_____State_____Zip_____

Telephone (   ) _____

A19BBABP

- -

Our Sunday Visitor
200 Noll Plaza
Huntington, IN 46750
Toll free: 1-800-348-2440
E-mail: osvbooks@osv.com
Website: www.osv.com